W  V

G000245526

What Happened Bridgie Cleary
A Play

Tom Mac Intyre

New Island/New Drama

WHAT HAPPENED BRIDGIE CLEARY
First published 2005
by New Island
2 Brookside
Dundrum Road
Dublin 14
www.newisland.ie

ISBN 1 904301 84 3

British Library Cataloguing in Publication Data. A CIP catalogue record for this book is available from the British Library.

Typeset by New Island
Cover image by Red Dog Design Consultants
Printed in Ireland by ColourBooks

New Island received financial assistance from
The Arts Council (An Chomhairle Ealaíon), Dublin, Ireland.

10 9 8 7 6 5 4 3 2 1

What Happened
Bridgie Cleary

By Tom Mac Intyre

The Abbey Theatre gratefully acknowledges
the financial support of The Arts Council
(An Chomhairle Ealaíon)

What Happened Bridgie Cleary

By Tom Mac Intyre

What Happened Bridgie Cleary by Tom Mac Intyre was first performed at the Abbey Theatre on 21 April 2005. Press night was 27 April 2005. Following its run at the Abbey Theatre, **What Happened Bridgie Cleary** toured nationally.

The performance runs for ninety minutes without an interval.

Cast in order of appearance

Bridgie Cleary	**Catherine Walker**
Mikey Cleary	**Tom Hickey**
William Simpson	**Declan Conlon**

Director	**Alan Gilsenan**
Designer	**Joe Vanek**
Lighting Designer	**Kevin McFadden**
Sound	**Cormac Carroll**
Voice Director	**Andrea Ainsworth**
Stage Director	**Audrey Hession**
Assistant Stage Manager	**Pamela McQueen**
Set	**Abbey Theatre Workshop**
Costumes	**Abbey Theatre Wardrobe Department**

Assistant to the Director	**Catherine McFadden**
Assistant to the Author	**Carla Braidin**
Director of the Peacock	**Ali Curran**

Please note that the text of the play which appears in this volume may be changed during the rehearsal process and appear in a slightly altered form in performance.

Tom Mac Intyre acknowledges his debt to Hubert Butler's seminal essay 'The Eggman and the Fairies', and *The Burning of Bridget Cleary: A True Story* by Angela Bourke.

The Abbey Theatre would like to thank Clare Hackett at the Guinness Storehouse for her help with this production.

Tom Mac Intyre Author

Tom Mac Intyre has written many plays for the Abbey
Theatre, most notably *The Great Hunger*, *Sheep's Milk on the
Boil* and *Good Evening Mr Collins*. His collaboration with
Tom Hickey – most recently in *The Gallant John-Joe* – is of
long standing.

Alan Gilsenan Director

Award-winning film-maker, writer and theatre director, Alan
Gilsenan's films include *The Road to God Knows Where*,
Prophet Songs, *Stories from the Silence*, *God Bless America*,
The Green Fields of France, *All Souls' Day*, *Private Dancer*,
Zulu 9, *The Irish Empire*, *Road II*, *The Ghost of Roger
Casement*, *Sing On Forever* and *Timbuktu*. For the theatre,
Gilsenan has directed Tom Murphy's *The Patriot Game* and
On the Outside/On the Inside for the Abbey Theatre, Jean
Genet's *The Balcony* and Tennessee Williams' *Small Craft
Warnings* for the Focus Theatre, *Hamlet* and Stephen
Berkoff's *Decadence* for the Naked Theatre, as well as his
own adaptation of John Banville's *The Book of Evidence* for
Kilkenny Arts Festival and the Gate Theatre.

Joe Vanek Designer

Joe Vanek's designs for major Abbey shows since 1990
include *Dancing at Lughnasa*, *Wonderful Tennessee*, *Observe
the Sons of Ulster Marching Towards the Somme*, *Angels in
America*, *Macbeth*, *The Secret Fall of Constance Wilde*, *St.
Joan*, *Love in the Title*, *Dolly West's Kitchen*, *Aristocrats* and
The Cherry Orchard.   Other recent designs include *Therese
Raquin*, *b.a.s.h*, *The Shape of Things*, *Gates of Gold*, Brian
Friel's *Performances* and *The Price* (Gate Theatre), David
Hare's *Skylight* and David Mamet's *Boston Marriage*
(Project), *Lady Macbeth of Mtsensk*, *The Silver Tassie* and
The Queen of Spades (Opera Ireland). Work abroad includes
By The Bog of Cats with Holly Hunter (USA), *Who's Afraid*

of Virginia Woolf? (Denmark) and the opera *The Makropulous Case* (Holland). Recent work includes *Enlightenment* (Peacock Theatre), David Bolger's *Nutracker* (CoisCéim Dance Theatre). Future plans include the Irish premiere of Edward Albee's *The Goat* for Landmark Productions at the Project in May. He has just co-curated the **abbey**onehundred: Scene Change Exhibition at the Irish Museum of Modern Art (IMMA) and was represented by four productions at the World Stage Design Exhibition in Toronto this March.

Kevin McFadden   Lighting Designer

Kevin's lighting design credits include *Taste* (Gúna Nua), *Romeo and Juliet* (Northside Theatre Company), *Bloody Poetry* (B.O.I. Arts Centre), *Seven Deadly Sins* (Performance Corporation). *The Guys* and *A Quiet Life* (Peacock Theatre).

Cormac Carroll   Sound Designer

Cormac is from Sligo. Companies worked for in Ireland include Bloc One Theatre, The Hawks Well Theatre and the Gaiety. As Sound Designer at the Abbey his work includes *Observe the Sons of Ulster Marching Towards the Somme, I Do Not Like Thee Doctor Fell, Heavenly Bodies, Defender of the Faith, Finders Keepers, Aristocrats, She Stoops to Conquer, The House of Bernarda Alba, All My Sons, The Plough and the Stars, Ariel, Da, Eden, Communion, The Guys, For the Pleasure of Seeing Her Again, The Memory of Water, The Sanctuary Lamp, Made in China* and *The Morning After Optimism*. His work for Rough Magic includes *Shiver, Olga, Words of Advice for Young People* and *Take Me Away.*

Declan Conlon   William Simpson

Declan's work at the Abbey and Peacock Theatres includes *Heavenly Bodies, All My Sons, Henry IV, A Whistle in the Dark, Famine, The Hamlet Project, The Last Ones* and *The*

Patriot Game. Other theatre work includes *Improbable Frequency*, *Copenhagen* (Rough Magic), *The Walls*, *The Ends of the Earth*, *The Machine Wreckers* (Royal National Theatre), *As You Like It*, *La Lupa*, *The Mysteries*, *The Spanish Tragedy*, *Henry VI Part III* (RSC), *Macbeth* (West End), *Our Country's Good* (Young Vic/Tour), *A Small Family Business*, *Amadeus* (Mercury Theatre, Colchester), *The Importance of Being Earnest* (Gate Theatre), *Juno and the Paycock* (Gaiety Theatre), *Decadence*, *Hamlet*, *Endgame* (Naked Theatre Company), *The Book of Evidence* (Kilkenny Arts Festival and Gate Theatre), *True West* (Lyric Theatre), *The Country* (Arklight Theatre Company), *The Sanctuary Lamp* (Manchester Royal Exchange) and *Jack and the Beanstalk* (the Gaiety pantomime). Television includes *Proof*, *Anytime Now*, *Bachelor's Walk*, *Hot House*, *Dangerfield* and *The Family*. Films include *Honest*, *All Souls' Day* and *Bite*.

Tom Hickey *Mikey Cleary*

Tom trained with Deirdre O'Connell at the Stanislavsky Studio and was a co-founder of the Focus Theatre. He has worked extensively at the Abbey Theatre since the seventies, creating leading roles in world premières of new Irish drama including *The Gigli Concert* by Tom Murphy, *Give Me Your Answer, Do!* by Brian Friel, *Observe the Sons of Ulster Marching Towards the Somme* by Frank McGuinness, *Misogynist* by Michael Harding, *The Silver Dollar Boys* by Neil Donnelly, *Portia Coughlan* and *By the Bog of Cats* by Marina Carr. He has had a close working relationship with Tom Mac Intyre for over twenty years. In the eighties he played in and collaborated with Mac Intyre and director Patrick Mason on several theatre-of-the-image plays, including the acclaimed *The Great Hunger* (which toured to Edinburgh, London, Paris, Moscow, Leningrad, New York), *The Bearded Lady*, *Rise Up Lovely Sweeney*, *Dance for Your Daddy* and *Snow White*. He directed that same author's *Sheep's Milk on the Boil* (Peacock, 1994) and *Chickadee* (Red

Kettle, 1993). His most recent collaboration with Tom Mac Intyre was the one-man play *The Gallant John-Joe*, which toured to Edinburgh, New York and many venues in Ireland, including the Aran Islands, having opened in Culdaff, County Donegal. Gate Theatre appearances include *Heartbreak House, Waiting for Godot, Aristocrats, Three Sisters, Double Dealer, A Midsummer Night's Dream, London Assurance, She Stoops to Conquer, Dorian Gray, Great Expectations, Stella by Starlight* and *Lady Windermere's Fan*. Films include *Flight of the Doves, Cal, To the Western World, Desecration, Gothic, High Spirits, My Left Foot, Nuns on the Run, Fools of Fortune, The Miracle, Raining Stones, Circle of Friends, Gold in the Streets, The Butcher Boy, The Last September, Coney Island Baby, Headrush, Inside I'm Dancing* and *Breakfast on Pluto*.

Catherine Walker   Bridgie Cleary

Catherine's theatre credits include Olivia in *Twelfth Night* (English Touring Theatre), Nora Reilly in *John Bull's Other Island* (Tricycle Theatre), Queen Isabelle in *Richard II*, Princess Katherine in *Henry V*, Vera in *A Month in the Country*, Cassandra in *Troilus and Cressida* (RSC), Amanda in *Wild Orchid* (Chichester Festival), The Girl in *Stairs to the Roof* (Minerva Theatre, Chichester), Sive in *Sive* (Tricycle and Palace Theatres) and Cordelia in *King Lear* (Second Age). Films include *Conspiracy of Silence, Passenger on Board* and *Sweeney Todd*. Television credits include Jodie Maxwell in *Holy City* and *The Favourite*. Catherine recorded *Scarlet Feather* by Maeve Binchy (Listening Books).

What Happened Bridgie Cleary by Tom Mac Intyre

National Tour June–July 2005

Town Hall Theatre, Galway
8–11 June

Backstage Theatre, Longford
15 and 16 June

Ramor, Virginia, Cavan
17 and 18 June

Garage Theatre, Monaghan
21 and 22 June

Town Hall, Dundalk
23 and 24 June

Mermaid Arts Centre, Bray
28 June–2 July

Earagail Arts Festival, An Grianán, Letterkenny
7–9 July

THE **ABBEY** THEATRE
Our warmest thanks go to:

Sponsors

Anglo Irish Bank

CityJet

Ferndale Films

RTÉ

The Gulbenkian Foundation

The Irish Times

The Sunday Tribune

Benefactors

Allied Irish Bank

An Post

Bank of Ireland

Behaviour & Attitudes
Marketing Research

Electricity Supply Board

Independent Newspapers
(Ireland) Limited

Irish Life and Permanent Plc

Pfizer International Bank
Europe

SIPTU

UniCredito Italiano Bank
(Ireland) Plc

Platinum Patrons

Allied Irish Bank, Upper
  O'Connell St Branch
Terry Calvani & Sarah Hill
Lilian & Robert Chambers
Diageo Ireland
Brian Halford
Donald Helme
Lorcan Lynch
Mercer Human Resource
  Consulting
Lorna Mooney
Andrew & Delyth Parkes
Alan Sheil
Derek Staveley
Adrian Timmons
Total Print & Design
Francis Wintle

Silver Patrons

Ron Butler
Joe Byrne
Zita Byrne
Orla Cleary
Claire Cronin
Maretti D'Arcy
Pauline Fitzpatrick
Monica Flood
Paul & Florence Flynn
Francis Keenan
Peter Keenan
Gerald Kelly & Co. Builders Providers
Ciaran Nicholson & David Lass
Mary T. Malone
Padraig McCartan
Mc Cullough – Mulvin Architects
Frank & Evelyn Murray
Vincent O'Doherty
John P.H & Rosemary O'Reilly
Sumitomo Mitsui Finance Dublin
Margaret Tallon
Michael Stein

Abbey Staff

What Happened Bridgie Cleary

Characters

Bridgie Cleary
Mikey Cleary
William Simpson

The piece is scored for uninterrupted performance of
ninety minutes' duration.

ACT ONE
SCENE ONE

Darkness. The sound of a sewing machine. The space gradually brightens. Bridgie is in her mid-twenties, modestly well-dressed and attractive. She is working at her sewing machine. The space is cheerless – everything seems sepia-tinted and has the atmosphere of a prison, although there's nothing overtly prison-like about it. The walls – canvas curtains – are flimsy. They stir and flap at intervals. There are a couple of bedraggled chairs in the space, as well as a makeshift table. We hear the wind at varying volumes, piano scales, and the croak of a heron – a plaintive blast – now and again.

Bridgie *hasn't looked up from her work yet. Now she looks up. There is something beautiful but strange about her. She stares incuriously at one point in the audience. She is very pale; everyone is pale in this climate. Silently, her finger tapping in support, she counts from one to ten.*

Bridgie You're thinkin', 'She's a prisoner ...' (*Pause.*) 'Bridgie's a prisoner ...' (*Pause.*) And *you're* not, I suppose? Muishe, isn't it well for you so, an' you not a prisoner – more power to you! *Treise leat, treise leat!*

She becomes irritated and returns to the sewing. There is a touch of recklessness to the pace, the vengeful even. She abandons the sewing again.

Bridgie Speakin' for meself, I never knew anyone that wasn't someway prisoner. The mother, God rest her,

had her prisoner tint, the father – bad scrant to him –
was what he was: born prisoner, an' he couldn't be
anniethin' else. Uncles, aunts, cousins, kissin' cousins –
all prisoners. (*Pause.*) No complaints. If ye complained,
what'd ye be complainin' for? That'd help? Would it?
Would it now? I never heard the Powers had much
time for whingers.

*She rises from the sewing machine with the shirt that she
has been sewing. She looks at the sewing machine and
caresses it idly.*

Bridgie The Singer. A mighty invinshin. I was the
first to have one on our patch of ground. The lot of
them said, 'That's her te the life. That's Bridgie. Always
a step or two above buttermilk. In her uppity breed
from God's Ould Time. Forever tryin' to put their arms
around the world. O, to be sure ... ' (*Pause.*) Well.
They had the clappin' tongues and they had the yalla
bile. I had the Singer – an' I was the one could make it
hum tunes. I'll warrant ye I was. I made weskits for the
gentry an' hats for the quality. (*Pause.*) That didn't
lessen the bile I can tell ye.

*She focuses suddenly on the shirt and stares at the bundle of
it in her hand. Opening the bundle with an odd
deliberation to her movements, she looks at the shirt. She
seems numb until she pulls the shirt apart with jerky
movements. She stares at the bits and pieces and tosses them
onto the table beside the machine, then wanders around the
space in a troubled fashion before sitting again. She
examines fretfully the fingernails of her left hand, then
recovers from the fret and relaxes.*

Bridgie The father used sing a song. He couldn't sing but he'd sing anyway when he'd a drop on him, always the one song, an' he'd crank it out two or three times a month, or a year – I do forget. But I remember the song. (*Pause.*) It was a song about a cow, a man milkin' a cow. An' one mornin' didn't the cow rear up, middle of the milkin', an' says the cow – that never uttered a word before – says she, 'That's it, for good an' all. No more milk will ye get from me.' (*Pause.*) I don't know how it was, or why, but I'd lie down and laugh fit te cry at the swagger o' that song. (*Pause.*) An' he had – no, it was the uncle, Uncle Beck, the half-twin, had one about a cow, another rebelly cow, cow that ett the piper. (*Pause, throwing the line away with a wicked edge.*) She'd a musical taste, th' unfortunate bayste ...

She pauses and focuses on the machine. She silently counts to ten and goes to the machine. Sitting down, she takes the pieces of shirt and in a ferocious burst of activity she begins sewing some of the pieces together again. The burst gradually cools and she becomes calm again, slowing the machine to a stop. She rests her elbows on the table of the machine and presses her joined hands against her forehead, with her head bowed. She goes perfectly still. A heron cries and the sound fades away. Eventually, **Bridgie** *looks up.*

Bridgie (*explaining*) Don't mind me at that, pass no heed. I do have to, certain times, go below that way – go in, an' go under. Just sway there, somewhere. I doubt it's encouraged; we're here te do sums, make discovrees, clarify gloom – but shure what matter? I do it annieways. I'll tell ye what'd put ye in mind of: yer stannin' above a pool, say, an' ye dive into yer reflection – that kinda thing. Get lost in yer own reflection. (*Long*

3

pause.) The which – *suspended* – exercise 'complished, yer free te return te yer (*long pause*) 'pointed duties. Drive on inta yer ... turmoils. (*Pause.*) Divil finds use, isn't that what they say, for stravaygin hands ...

She rises and walks like a prisoner in a cell, then relaxes and sits again. Smiling to herself, she mimes a farm-hand milking a cow, and a conspirator's gleam comes over her. She jumps up suddenly and kicks over the chair. Now she is the cow.

Bridgie 'No more milk will ye get from me!' (*She smiles.*) It's called "The Risin", like '98 – The Year o' Liberty – that came an' went. (*Beat.*) An' talkin' o' cows, the mother had a sayin'. She'd say, 'Y'know, that's like a night a cow might calve.' More nor well put, I often thought ... Maynin'? (*She rights the chair.*) Maynin', I suppose, some marvel hangin' in the air, marvel past addin' or subtractin'. Nights come like that, gentle nights ye'd smell promise, promise o' some grand yield altogether in the quiet o' trees.

She returns to the Singer and touches it almost reverentially.

Bridgie The shirt (*she gestures at it resting on the Singer*) is for a particler party – times I remember, times I don't. It's a shirt hard to compose, all things considered. And there's a pinnyfore (*she takes one from the drawer of the Singer*) for someone's child. It won't come right an' I get vexed with the size, the curl of a letter, letter S for Susannah. It's s'posed te be put-a-name-on, ye see, an' the colour, times I swop the colour. Couldn't unravel the whim if ye asked me, but the hanky (*she takes a blue hanky from her pocket*) – the

hanky *will* come right, I know and do believe. Don't
let on te the tree or the moss on the stone – the hanky
o' blue is for the one soul I ever kem across that wasn't
no prisoner, only, lek many another, I didn't, at the
time, have enough wit te see it. Didn't have the wit.
(*Pause.*) At that time.

There is a long pause. Bridgie oils the Singer.

Bridgie   Look after what matters. An' what's that –
what matters? What matters. Wren-bird belongin' te
these parts – birds is great messengers – this wren told
me, 'What matters, Bridgie, is the *real work.*' 'An'
what's the real work?' I made bould te ask. The real
work – I was advised – is *what's te be done.* (*Pause.*)
There y'are now. (*Pause.*) Real work. (*Beat.*) *What is te
be done.*

*She gives the Singer a run, then stops it and adjusts the
bobbin.*

Bridgie   Bobbins is quare gazayboes, lek they were
made te hop – won't easily suffer confinement. Ye'd
have a soft spot for the poor craythurs, jiggin' away
there in their giddy confinemen'.

Bridgie *puts the lid back on and picks imaginary fluff from
her dress.*

Bridgie   Bridgie Cleary, who made weskits for the
gentry, hats for the quality. Bridgie Cleary, always the
step or two above buttermilk, comes from Ballyvadlea
in the County Tipperary, at the fut of Slievenamon.
(*Beat.*) Slievenamon. (*Beat.*) At the fut of Slievenamon.

SCENE TWO

The transition is carried by partial dimming of the lights and a gradual return to normal light values.

Bridgie (*automaton*) 'Are you a witch or are you a fairy/Or are you the wife of Mikey Cleary?/ I'm no witch, nor am I fairy/I was once wife to a Mikey Cleary ...'

Bridgie *slowly raises a hand to her right ear and inserts a finger, almost in slow motion. She slowly turns her little finger in the ear around and around, then removes the finger.*

Bridgie Windin' the clock, I calls it, which is a foolishness. There's no clocks here – but there is *time*, funny enough. Only what is it? Oh, it's lots o' things – I'm the one can tell yiz that. Sometimes it's a big navy blue gansy, knittin' itself, then ravellin', then knittin' itself over again. Other times I see it an' it's lek nothin' so much as a frog in a frost, all scrunched up an' sighin' to itself. Other times – arrah, ye couldn't be goin' on about it – it knows too much.

She repeats the routine with her left ear, then picks at imaginary fluff and arranges her dress about her lap.

Bridgie Lisnin', ye know, can be put up te ye in a wicked way too. In a former time I'd dream often where I'd be takin' skelps of wax from one ear or t'other. That was a warnin', an' one got little heed. But I begin, *begin*, te understan' that lisnin' an' heedin' are matters of consequence. (*Pause.*) And silence, there's another *glic* one. (*Pause.*) Certainly, silence. There's silence can deafen – not many knows that. I heard tell of a young lad – lighthouse keeper – out Ardmore way or Helvick Head, could be, and, there too long on his own, didn't he go deaf, young enough now, from the volume o' silence. They brought him to a healer – useless – it was gone far too far inta chambers of the ear. The healer, not but he'd a wide inheritance of woeful skills, he couldn't find his way next or near the roots of that young fella's interdickshin.

The wind snaps at the curtains.

Bridgie (*dreamy echo*)   'Never a witch, never a fairy/Sometime married to a man called Cleary ...'

Her head is nodding slowly now and her lips are moving as if she is counting. **Mikey** *enters the space. He is over sixty and dressed in peasant-tradesman garb. He carries a sack with his carpentry tools.*

Bridgie, *in a downstage position, is unaware of his presence.* **Mikey** *stands there and takes off his cap. He makes to say something but doesn't, and puts his cap back on. He advances.* **Bridgie** *is now aware of his presence.* **Mikey** *sits, and there is a rattle of tools as he sets down his sack.* **Bridgie** *studies him.*

Bridgie   Who might you be?

No answer.

Bridgie   You were asked a question. Bothered ears?

Mikey I don't know.

Pause.

Bridgie Doesn't know who he is ...

Mikey I don't know, I said. Let me get a hould o' meself, will ye?

Pause.

Bridgie The way with lots, I s'pose.

Mikey Entirely right. Way with lots.

Bridgie *studies him.* **Mikey** *frowns sharply. He studies the audience resentfully. He takes off his cap and plants it on his knee.* **Bridgie** *rises and tours the space, circling him. She halts.*

Bridgie Yer scattered – on the head of a journey. As a result, not capable of knowin' who ye might be? That be to be it?

Mikey I'm scattered all right. (*Beat.*) I'll return to meself, never fret.

He looks at her, giving nothing, but the audience can sense that he's finding his bearings. **Bridgie**, *getting stronger all the time, circles him again. She is keeping her distance but gaining in authority.*

Bridgie Well, ye needn't fret about not knowing who y'are. It'll catch up with ye. Very few escapes. Them's the lucky ones, it's said.

Mikey *looks at her. He is already the accused, invariably the accused.*

Mikey An' you, when y'are at home, you're ...?

Bridgie You've no call te ask that. You can tell who y'are now. I can tell ye know who y'are. (*Pause.*) An' ye can tell – if ever man could tell – ye can tell who's the woman fornenst ye. So yev landed, have ye? Mikey. What age did ye last te, tell us?

Mikey Sixty-five – or 'ithin an ass's roar of it.

Bridgie Ye look more. Ye always looked more than ye were. That's how ye were spoken of: 'Look for a man who luks far older nor he is. Touch of an interior stoop.' Sixty-five. Near enough the three-score-an'-ten. Well, ye had a good ould whack of it, Mikey Cleary, sight more nor lots is given. No sign ye discovered any great mirth comin' down the hill – but shure maybe that wasn't laid out for ye. Did ye hear what I'm after sayin', Mikey Cleary? Well, divil the much change in one thing annieways. Ye never wasted a word if stitched lips'd do nicely.

Pause.

Mikey Bridgie –

Bridgie Yes, Mikey Cleary?

Mikey I was half-expectin' te see ye.

Bridgie Well. People meet an' the hills don't.

Mikey Where are we here, Bridgie?

Bridgie *Here's* ... where we are. Nowhere else.

Mikey Free to come an' go?

Bridgie Free to wake up. Wake. Up.

Mikey Free to wake up?

Bridgie If so minded. Free to doze, I s'pose, if that's th'appetite ...

Mikey Are we looked after, itself?

Bridgie Looked after? (*She smiles.*) Not *over*looked, say ...

Mikey A prison, is it? Another prison?

Bridgie Show me the spot there's no chains.

Mikey What's (*he tilts his head*) outside there?

Bridgie Nuthin'. Everythin'. Have a luk. Ye won't get far.

Mikey *decides to leave it there.*

Mikey 'People meet an' the hills don't' – didn't hear that sayin' with years.

Mikey *takes a box of ointment from his pocket, opens it awkwardly and rubs ointment on each of his palms in turn.* **Bridgie** *watches this activity, interested, not interested.*

Mikey I'm crucified with a skin ailmen' on the palms o' the hand.

Pause. He works in the ointment.

Mikey Got it when they had me sewin' mail-bags – God spare us – years back.

Bridgie Palms of the hand does be a delicate zone.

Mikey Sometimes it withdraws, but not for long. They've a name for it, only I forget. A Red Injun I kem across tuk on te clear it – an' tuk a fistful o' money from me – but he turned out a fraud. Which I shudda known from the start. He was blind of one eye. An' a furra down the middle of his forehead ye could grow cabbage in. (*Pause.*) The whore's melt was one lopsided fraud.

Bridgie Red Injun.

Mikey Aye.

Bridgie Where was this goin' on? Ye didn't meet a Red Injun at the fair o' Mullinahone?

Mikey Canada.

Bridgie Canada.

Mikey Spent me days in Canada after. Cooperin'. I had me trade.

Bridgie *After*. A dayle o' churnin' in that word – *after* ...

Mikey After the jail. I was thrown in jail – with a few more – an' others got off that should be in jail till crocodiles teks up tin-whistles, but I was clapped inside for somethin' was no doin' o' mine. In th'end, I'm let loose. Spent rest o' me days in Canada. Cooper can always get work. I had me trade.

Bridgie *moves about the space, preoccupied, vaguely tidying. She alters the position of a chair and needlessly rearranges the set of the lid on the Singer.*

Mikey Bridgie –

She gives no heed.

Mikey Bridgie –

She ignores him and continues her activity.

Mikey I've a thing to say, Bridgie.

Bridgie No hurry on ye.

Mikey I've a thing to say –

Bridgie Yer in a great chasm o' space here, as ye'll discover. Take yer hour, I told ye. (*Beat.*) Then ye might find yev nuthin' to say – 'cept maybe to yerself – to a noise passing, to levels of serenity, fer essample, goin' to-an'-fro in the broad surround. Takes gettin' te know. Then, as I menchind, there's no hurry in this commodyus air.

*It's all too much for **Mikey** and he goes into himself.*

Bridgie *fusses over the two or three apertures in the containing curtain flaps that pass for doors. She adjusts the lie of them slightly, looks out, and soothes once again the hang of the curtains. She wanders to a seated position and talks to the audience, paying no heed to* **Mikey**, *who sits there, attending morosely, like a perennial stranger.*

Bridgie   One thing you'd miss is doors. If it was only a place, a frame, te stand in, and luk out at whatever'd be te te be seen. Or half-door, even, te lean on. Never thought you'd find me missin' a half-door. Or the small pleasure of closin' a door – you'd miss that too. I'd great time for a door ajar, why'd that be now? Or light – lights, maybe – showing from under a door. And the mother'd go on about 'The Spotty Door' – that's the door in the side of Slievenamon has a dose of traffic. Wander through there, mishap or intended, yer with them belongs te a diffren' world. 'The Spotty Door.' Often wondered what it looked like. Exactly. Could find out yet, I s'pose. Door with freckles – who'd imagine that now?

Mikey   Great weather for young ducks, great weather for young ducks.

Bridgie (*to the audience*)   I got a class of a glimpse once, an' no more nor a glimpse, of what's stirrin' behind that Spotty Door. I was walkin' te the school-house one mornin'. I was late but ye'd get away with late if ye were under five.

Mikey   Yer ould slope o' the mountain, come down oura that, will ye?

13

Bridgie *roams the space, performing the upcoming event. Her movement is close to a dance.*

Bridgie   Under five ye were granted liberty. So, I was meandrin' te school, October mornin', that or November, takin' the short-cut, the meado's, and of a sudden I'm walkin' in them webs an' tangles o' gossamer, glintin' threads an' drops everywhere, an' it was like I never had to part a single strand – they'd lift or melt away – so's I could slide through, I never – to my best information – was hitmatised be an expert in that art, but this mornin' – an', tell the truth, long as I was in it, I had layve te move in another place nor the come-day-go-day, an' that's one reason word *gossamer*'s special for me, likely I was bound te be a dress-maker after that, magickin' gossamer stuff, silks, satins, and so on, the smooth feel of – *downy* items – ye'd encounter. It was me christenin', ye might say, that spun-silver mornin'.

Pause.

Mikey   Martyr me, Mary, sideways slowly ...

Bridgie   Aye, I was allowed a christenin' with a differ, ye might say, that spun-silver mornin'.

SCENE THREE

Change to low-key lighting to carry transition. **Mikey** *is seated as before, in a downstage position.* **Bridgie** *is seated at the Singer again, her hand resting on the lid of the machine.* **Mikey** *focuses on the bag of tools. He picks it up and takes out a saw, a hammer, and bits of timber.*

Mikey   A trade is what gives a man dignity. I was a cooper all me days.

Piano scales intrude. **Mikey** *falls silent. The piano scales, modestly tyrannical, complete their sequence.*

Mikey   Thanks be te God, I had me trade.

Piano scales intrude again.

Mikey   Will ye give over an' let a body spake?

Bridgie (*coming to life brightly*)   Don't bark at them notes, might be glad o' them yet –

Piano scales continue, implacably.

Mikey (*furious*)   Ye ditch's get ye, can ye not pitch yer cavorshins somewhere ye won't be heard?

Bridgie   See? He'll never be gainsaid be Bridgie.

Piano scales continue uninterrupted and fade away in their own good time.

15

Mikey Cooperin' all me days. Best at me trade on the bockety slopes of the mountain. People could look at a firkin – butter te the brim – an' say – 'Mikey Cleary med that firkin, ye'd know be the cut of it.' Just the same as ye'd tell a good tailor be the lie o' the garment. That's (*he displays a piece of timber*) proper sayzoned oak; it's useless if it's not aged right. She'll warp, split, rot overnight, laugh at ye from the *smidiríní*.

Bridgie How d'ye know a cooper's yard convaynyent? The sun-up te sun-down hammerin'. An' the ojious smell. It'd pewk ye. I had a cat – beauty without paint – got sick more nor once from them inflickshins.

Mikey, *heedless, throws the piece of timber aside.*

Mikey The cooperin's not a bad livin'. Firkins. Tubs. Barrels. Always be a demand. They'd tell ye in Canada machines'll take over. I wouldn't give the shakin's o' me piss for Canada. 'The scum o' Europe,' heard a man sayin' once, 'The scum o' Europe.' Doan ever put a foot near Canada unless yer in manacles, that'd be my advice. Mounties. Frenchmen. Ointmen'-haired Red Injuns. Dirty snow an' black ice. Ye wouldn't put a crow-bar out in it.

He rises wearily, eyes **Bridgie**, *and listens. The piano scales, as though mocking him, play in diminuendo before fading.*

Bridgie (*she's been listening*)   Arrah, don't go. Often wanted to learn a piana ... (*Listening again.*) *What hurry's on ye?*

Mikey (*standing mid-stage, making a pronouncement*)   I

16

wasn't responsible for anniethin' ever happened,
Bridgie. But I know, an' there's lots more nor me
knows, the insides of the harm wuz dun ye. (*Pause.*)
There wuz a bad mistake the first day – the buildin' o'
that house on a fairy-fort. I spoke agin that. The pack
was in it before us, The Long Leahys, was druv from it,
noises in the night, an' the hullabaloo lets ye know The
Beyond Crowd is about the spot. Will somewan passin'
the road tell me, what entered *us*, goin' near the place
an' the bad blasht history of it plain te see? I spoke
agin it at the time. Only I was overcome in the
argufyin': 'Shur isn't it a gran' house. Don't be listenin'
to *fawsteem* and pishogues!' That was, my opinion, the
start o' the bother. Advancin' into a house, a marked
house, was built on a fairy-fort.

*He walks to the perimeter of the space like a prisoner
walking his cell. He stops downstage and stares at* **Bridgie**.
Her dreamy focus is on the audience. **Mikey** *walks slowly
up to her and stands beside her. His tension is percussive.*

Mikey Bridgie?

Bridgie I heard of a pianist gev a concert once in
Clonmel. An Eyetalyan-soundin' name he had.

Pause.

Mikey (*giving up, walking away singing a soul-song to
himself*) Bridgie, Bridgie, Bridgie Cleary ... Maybe
I'm a class of a wandrin' Jew that flung the boot at
Christ an' had te travel roads ever after – an' no one te
listen to his complainin's.

Bridgie Name like *Bianconi*, only more song to it. *Clementini*, was it – *Signor Clementini?*

Mikey Bridgie Cleary was a woman unwell. Petitioner states the Doctor attendin' his wife Bridgie wasn't to be had when needed, resultin' in her fever spreadin' when no need for same, an', worse nor that, when he did consint te appear, tin days later, presented himself in an alcoholic confusion, as a progression of which he wuz in no fit state to stutoscope symptoms of patient, wife te Mikey Cleary, as witnessed before, an', on top of all, was abusive te said Mikey Cleary an' te newmress others besides, an, latter end, leaves the premises without expressin' no concern for the patient nor annie o' them envolved. Furthermore, an' te conclude, the same Medical Ossifer was known across the seven parishes te be wild as a hatchet from the day he was weaned, an' drunk as a stick on most of his rounds.

Bridgie If I'd me chance agin, I believe I'd learn a piana – play, maybe, in fine houses, company'd be a blind harper ... Why was them harpers blind, there's one for ye?

Mikey *moves to an extreme downstage position. He holds his left hand extended, palm upward, and beats his left palm repetitively with his right index finger. The wind intrudes and snaps at the curtain, whines, and wanders off.* **Mikey**, *having delayed for silence, speaks, his index finger beating his left palm.*

Mikey Mikey Cleary was a man loved his lawful wife Bridgie. An', moreover – a man never rested finger on

18

another woman – nor annie urge te same – even in the
early years when the two were livin' apart, him residin'
in Clonmel owin' te the demands o' his trade. Mikey
Cleary seen the harm dun up an' down the road from
carry-on the lek o' that, childer without names or only
half-names lukin' through every hole in a hedge. An'
good reputayshins left in flitthers. Say what yiz like of
him, Mikey Cleary was never a man led be his tool.

He goes up to **Bridgie** *and stands beside her. Her half-smile
plays lightly on the audience.* **Mikey** *extends a wavering
hand; he has a mind to touch her. His hand floats there.*

Bridgie Why was them harpers blind – there's a
qwanundrum? Were they blinded be the music, d'ye
fancy? Stranger things happens, I s'pose. Or did they
give in te the music, light gone from their eyes?
(*Pause.*) That happens too, be all accounts ...

Mikey *withdraws the hand and drifts downstage again. He
sits and removes his battered boots.*

Mikey We were gettin' on well in the day-to-day,
there was no cause for bother, none in the wide world.
She had all she ever wanted, the dress-makin' an' the
millinry, an' her well in charge of herself at them trades.
I had the cooperin' an' more work nor I could keep up
with. There was no ill-will, no bargin', no gernin' of
any description between the pair of us. Lots tried to
mek play of there bein' a lack o' childer. The which was
only ould guff. Lack o' childer didn't bother her, didn't
bother me – we knew the childer'd come when s'posed
to come, there was no hurry on us – what hurry'd be
on us an' us a young an' thrivin' couple?

Pause. The sound of a heron croaking brashly and wind flaps. These sounds rise, fall, and fade. **Mikey** *looks upstage.* **Bridgie,** *light-fingered, is 'playing the piano' at the Singer.* **Mikey** *looks at the audience. Fatigue fills him. He props his head up with an elbow on one knee and seems to be emptying himself into the cap of the audience. Strong odours of self-pity.* **Bridgie** *rises in slow motion from her position at the Singer. Now there's a seductive flowering, an intoxicating colour to her movements. Seemingly in a trance, she works a brief haunting reprise of the choreography which accompanied her gossamer story in the preceding scene.* **Mikey** *watches, phrases from his account of the lack of children breaking from him.*

Bridgie (*from her trance/dance*) Gossamer ... Yer goose-summer gossamer ... An' Michaelmas ...

Mikey Lack o' childer didn't bother her wan damn bit.

Bridgie The Michaelmas goose-summer gossamers, tanglin' the webs o' the dew on what's left o' the leaves ...

Mikey Didn't bother her, didn't bother me ...

Bridgie The leaves an' the scutch-grass and thrawneens o' branches could tell ye yer name ...

Mikey What hurry'd be on us an' us a young an' thrivin' couple?

Bridgie That's the goose-summer gossamer o' Michaelmas, *ól suas é*, a mornin's mornin', sun on yer

back, you makin' yer way be the path through the
eider-down stir o' the meado's ...

Mikey Talk of a lack o' childer was only ould guff.

Bridgie *returns to her Singer position. The space settles.*
Mikey *rouses himself again.*

Mikey Said Mikey Cleary, formerly resident of
Ballyvadlea, County Tipperary, an', at a later date, of
Montreal, Canada, abovementioned states villain o' the
proceedings, the one – as is openly assepted – caused
all the calamtees was the lispin' snarlygob Dunne, one
Jack Dunne, a festrin' crab with a sackful o' cures an'
charms and twisted ribbons from May Eve, he was the
wan landed in on us, meself an' a few dacent relations
an' consarned neighbours, we attindin' my ailin' wife,
only *he* lights on top of us, his own Mid-Night Nurse
an' Captain Moonlight, with orders an' instructions,
hitmatised everyone present, swearin' black oaths it's
not Bridgie is in it, there's changelin' work stirrin', she's
bin whipped away, it's *not her is in it*, she's two inches
taller, *it's not her is in it* –

Single piano scale, clinically neutral. **Bridgie** *listens,
attentive.*

Bridgie That man – best day he was in it – 'd never
listen te the notes. Tunes in the nettle if ye care te
listen. In dandylions. Inside the rain. Buckets o' tunes.
Only ye have te listen.

Mikey (*furious*) Jack Dunne – whose story before the
Judge was chaptered perjuries for which may he rot in

whatever eternity is now his crusted bed – Dunne was the wan, rank seed in him, who whispered it te the kitchen gang: 'Shure weren't her people' – maynin' Bridgie – 'weren't they all the little bit, away, y'know' – an' found lots te listen, and wasn't that same pookwubberoon the one drochooled them and keodreeched them, an' when he had them frothin', the procession o' them in that kitchen, he was the one gev the command, rasp o' Satan in the cracked windpipe of him – 'Put down a good fire – we'll make her answer!' – an' the bad work went on from there. People loses possession of themselves, *imithe ar strae*, all's changed.

The piano plays a few bars of 'Slievenamon'. **Bridgie** *draws attention to it, gesturing for people to listen.*

Bridgie (*reciting*)   The hall it is gay an' the waves they are grand/But my heart is not here at all/It flies far away be night an' be day/To the time an' the joys that are gone/An' I never can forget the sweet maiden I met/In the valley of Slievenamon.

SCENE FOUR

Lighting change carries transition to next scene. **Mikey,** *in spite of himself, listens to the piano notes. He is alerted to* **Bridgie**'s *commencing activity by the Singer. She removes the lid and, with a zeal touched by the frenetic, starts working on the shirt again. Abruptly, she halts the work.*

Bridgie   Mikey Cleary –

He looks at her and nods.

Bridgie (*sternly*)   Ye'll have te study how not t'intrude on me. Bridgie Cleary's not for queschinin'. I've, this long while, me own circles drawn te steady me balance in these dominions. So. I want that unnerstud. Save vexation for all parties.

Mikey   All right so. That's yer entitlemen'. I'd no wish te be bargin' at ye. Only there was a certain few items –

Bridgie   *That'll do –*

Her tone brings him to heel. She resumes work. **Mikey** *now views his tools of labour, and gets to work in turn, but there's a desultory beat to his foosterings with bits of timber and other instruments.* **Bridgie,** *even while she's at the Singer, inspects his motions. She now allows the machine to come to a stop.*

Bridgie   Ye gev up the cooperin' a long time ago? Didn't make a firkin with a month o' years, did ye?

23

Mikey That's the truth, now ye say it.

Bridgie The hands.

Mikey (*nodding*) Hands wouldn't let me. Had te give it up.

Bridgie An' yer fresh occupation?

Mikey I got work as a sort of a watchman, mindin' one of them big warehouses be night.

Bridgie I could tell when ye spoke o' the cooperin' ye were peddlin' patent dalla-mullogue. (*Pause.*) Ye were always a poor liar, Mikey Cleary. Do yer best but never had the honey tongue for that recreation.

The two just float there.

Mikey I missed the cooperin'. Ye miss what yer custom'd te. A warehouse be night is the wind gulderin', an' noises from nowhere.

Bridgie Like here. Wind gulderin', noises from nowhere ...

Long pause. **Mikey** *morosely examines a bit of timber.* **Bridgie** *gives the Singer a whirl but tires of it.*

Bridgie My father'd be long dead, I suppose, God rest him.

No response from **Mikey**, *who is tossing all the neglected bits and pieces back into the sack.*

Bridgie   Did his best while he was let. Only the mother was the one for me. I wouldn't speak agin him. But the mother was the one for me.

Mikey   I stopped a man once on a street o' Montreal, and sez I to him, 'How would a man get rid of a pair o' ailin' hands?' 'Go to a doctor.' Tried them all, I tould him. 'Yer sure it's just ailin' hands is in it?' sez he. And away with him, lek he never was ...

Bridgie   Aye, great time for the mother.

Pause.

Mikey   All knew that.

Bridgie   Did they now?

Mikey   All knew that.

Bridgie   Did you?

Mikey   To be sure, I did.

Bridgie   An' it bothered ye?

Mikey   Never said that.

Bridgie   Thought it maybe?

Mikey   Thoughts come aisy.

Bridgie   So it did bother ye?

Mikey Aequal te me, whether ye med much of her, little of him. Much of him, little of her. Aequal te me.

Pause.

Bridgie Ye found her strange, maybe?

Mikey Never said that.

Bridgie Well, maybe she found you strange – that ever tread the corrugations of yer mind?

Mikey Once or twice maybe. She wasn't the most conversable. There was a remove to her. A distant quiet.

Bridgie And that was bad, was it? The distant quiet in her?

No reply.

Bridgie Lots of women I met on me road had a distant quiet in them. Best of their play, maybe. But you were never greatly drawn to the women, were ye? Work. Work. The head down. Mikey Cleary wouldn't stop te piss, 'twas said. Open the britches, work away, souse the sod, work away, button britches, work away. Wouldn't stop te piss.

No reply.

Bridgie Man tould me once an ould sayin' he had, picked it up somewhere, 'Wherever ye land, always make sure ye have the women on yer side.'

Mikey, *for an answer, takes off a woollen sock and massages a big toe without pleasure. He puts the sock on again.* **Bridgie** *remains immobile.*

Mikey Ye do have yer hands full at the Singer.

Bridgie *takes the shirt, the pinafore from the drawer, and the blue hanky from her pocket. She comes downstage to engage* **Mikey,** *engage but keep her distance. She is not at all relaxed and there is a sense of the lonesome, the burdened about her. She displays the items.*

Bridgie The shirt's for you is my unnerstannin' but it won't come aisy. I'm supposed te work at it. Pinnyfore's for the daughter of a neighbour – if I keep at it ye never could tell ... The blue hanky's for (*mischief rising in her*) a select one I used meet down the road. 'One for the master, one for the maid, and one for a lad lives down the lane.' (*Beat.*) It'll come right, I do believe – the blue hanky.

Pause.

Mikey The pinnyfore's for one of William Simpson's young lassies, that be the case?

Bridgie That's right.

Mikey A terror the things a body remembers. Them two gearcailes – what's it their names was?

Bridgie Susannah an' Denise, wasn't it?

Mikey Susannah, aye, and Denise. That Susannah

chile had the quare eye in her head. She'd luk at ye, an' ye wouldn't know from stray turnips what'd be crossin' her mind.

Bridgie That's the women, Mikey Cleary ...

Mikey Martyr me, Mary, sideways slowly ...

Bridgie We're an inward species.

Mikey Too inward for the lek o' me. But whether or which, that chile, if I'm not mixin' her up, she'd always luk at me lek she thought I'd a sod gone from the load.

Pause.

Bridgie Whatever became of the brave William?

Mikey He'll luk after himself, wherever he is.

Bridgie William was all right.

Mikey Ye'd always a wakeness for the swanks, Bridgie Cleary.

Bridgie Nothin' wrong with being choosy.

Mikey Not a damn thing, not a damn thing. O, Christ, no.

Bridgie What age would he be now? William ...

Mikey I'd never trust a landlord's agent. A land-grabber. An' a prize canat, if ever ye live to meet one.

And the moustache. He'd this little comb for it. If ye seen him, workin' the midget comb on the trained moustache.

Bridgie (*easy*) That's right. Ye'd foal watchin'. (*She mimes* **William** *combing the moustache, milking the image.*) And the cut-away collar ... (*She mimes him checking his looks in a mirror.*) Never happier than coortin' a mirror, there's men lek that. An' the prancin' of him. Shure what harm, he was good te me. A woman values a degree o' pettin'. (*Pause.*) He had a kindness, if ye agreed to coax it inta the light o' day.

Pause. **Mikey** *is festering.*

Bridgie Be a tidy age now, William. And I liked them two little gearcailes. The wife used crowshay, so's she wouldn't have te lift her head, people said. Timid bundle she was, the same Hesther.

Mikey A gran' couple, the Simpsons. Livin' off the backs o' the poor an' th'evicted. Damn lucky he wasn't shot from his horse – I saved him two or three times. Stud up for him – whatever possessed me. I wuddent do it again.

The Singer whirrs into independent life, treats itself to a good gallop. There's an odd sense in which it seems to be talking in secret language to **Bridgie**. **Mikey**, *forever looking for his bearings, doesn't miss that. The Singer completes its gallop, with* **Bridgie** *seeming to nurse it into contented silence.*

Mikey Does it talk too?

Bridgie I do have te tell it te shut up, would ye believe? Still an' all, brings me newses, newses of – private matters. Mighty number (*patting the Singer*), aren't ye? Mighty number.

Pause.

Mikey Are we here forever?

Bridgie What would you say now yourself?

Mikey We won't get outa this jail.

Bridgie Sometimes I think –

Mikey We'll be offered parole, is it?

Bridgie Sometimes, sometimes I wonder is people … given a second gallop, lek books goes on about.

Mikey A second gallop? Pray Christ we're spared that!

Bridgie I dunno. Depinds, I s'pose. All depinds.

Mikey Depinds on what?

Bridgie On – on the weather shapin' inside ye. After a while here ye'd say, 'Could be that's what they're after?'

Mikey '*They*' – who's '*they*' when they're at the garden gate, tell us?

Bridgie Who's '*they*'? Th' Other Crowd, Mikey Cleary, Th' Other Crowd.

Mikey Jesus spare us an' protect us.

Bridgie If yer not given a second gallop, I'm provoked te wonder what's the journeyin' for – journeyin' down below, then more here – of an inward kind, I mayne. What I'm sayin' is I get the smell o' schoolin' somewhere in th'entertainment, an' that's why I do be thinkin' is a second gallop – aye, an' lots o' gallops, come to that – a permitted part o' the bargain?

Mikey *Bargain!*

Bridgie Could occur. Could occur an' never happen.

Mikey *Bargain*, says she.

Pause.

Mikey Does others come by itself?

Bridgie You're the first – first made visible, annieways. But – layvin' people out of it – there's no scarcity o' traffic, from one-steps te processions, ye'd hear it shiftin' around. Get used te it. How much it knows is hard te say. But – if I'm not greatly misled – it pays heed. This is *The Land*, I decided after a while, of *The Secret Intinshin* – yer s'posed te root out yer *Secret Intinshin* that was, an' is. An' then do what? Sing it, I s'pose. Or – or – *be it*. Or – or – ye'll be told. Sometime or other.

Mikey '*Secret Intinshin*'?

Bridgie *won't pursue it. She focuses on the blue hanky,* *smells it, feels the texture, folds it, makes a flower of it, plays that flower against her hand.*

Bridgie   Ye remember the Egg-Man?

En garde look from **Mikey.** **Bridgie** *is roaming the space, becoming excited.*

Bridgie   Is yer memory shattered, Mikey Cleary?

Mikey   I remember him all right.

Bridgie's *wanderings have left her upstage right as she commences the Egg-Man riff.* **Mikey** *is restively downstage right, restive but on the* qui vive. **Bridgie** *is the one who has freedom to move, to perform. She's now availing of it. She focuses on an imaginary figure downstage left and her cantata to the Egg-Man will take her slowly along the diagonal to the well-nigh audible frisson of arrival.*

Bridgie   Ye remember I had a batch o' hens. Wyandottes, Rhode Island Reds. Fine laying hens. I sold a rake of eggs. Weekly. The Egg-Man'd come, I'd be waiting for him, eggs cleaned an' shinin'. I'd present them te him, an' get good money for them. Best of eggs they were too.

Mikey   O, from you he'd get nuthin' but the best, I knows that.

Bridgie   Phildy Reddan. He was from beyond Ballingarry, place called Coroneary. And he was free as a bird. An' eye in his head. Watch him arrivin' an' ye'd say, 'This fella's step must draw sparks from the splinc o' the road.' That kind o' step. His father was a piper.

Mikey 'Phil, Phil, the piper's son/Stole a pig an' away did run.'

Bridgie Wonder what ever became of him ...

Mikey 'The pig was ett, and Phil was bet/Phil, Phil the piper's son.'

Bridgie 'D'ye play the pipes, Phildy?' I asked him wance. 'I plays all instruments known,' sez he. 'I'm finger-gifted, Bridgie, juz lek you.'

Pause.

Mikey What'd the women see in that tramp? He'd mount the break o' day.

Bridgie Phildy Reddan ...

Mikey Cat goin' through a sky-light ...

Bridgie (*flourishing the hanky again*) This is for him, was I tellin' ye?

Mikey Ye were. Now yer tellin' me the twict.

Bridgie Little bit of a thing, but of my makin'.

Mikey Sort of a *charm* it'd be to be, that what yer sayin'?

Bridgie I like that blue ...

Mikey So long as I'm not put a spell on.

Bridgie That blue is *him*, some way or other. Not turquoise, but it comes close. Told him once he'd eyes more turquoisey nor ever I saw.

Mikey Jewels, is it, 'stead of bloodshot windas lek the rest of us mortals?

Bridgie *There* was a man was doin' what he was s'posed te be doin' ...

Mikey Lek mountin' my wife.

Bridgie Chattin' people. Handlin' eggs. With the soft of his hands. Hens. Ye'd always see a feather, reddy-brown, maybe, somewhere on his person. Very first time I saw him, I told him, 'Phildy, Phildy Reddan, ye shouldn't be let loose.' 'Why so, Bridgie Cleary?' sez he, an' the cap as usual on the Kildare side, avick. 'Why so?' 'Because,' I tould him, 'yer one livin' danger.' An' the laugh of him. Feckshis laugh he had. Ye'd have liked him, if ye'd had the chance to know other more. We used talk lots of ye, y'know.

Mikey That's what the women always sez – an' them swoppin' wan tool for another: 'Shure we talk mostly o' you.'

Bridgie I think he'd a good unnerstannin' o' ye. He *knew* people, some way or other.

Mikey An' that musta been a great help. On top o'
his other endowmen's ...

Bridgie *is quite unperturbed by this swipe. She is back by
the Singer, a provocative gleam in her eye. She flourishes, in
quick succession, the shirt, the pinafore, and the hanky.*

Bridgie One for the master ...

Mikey Wasn't there talk o' geldin' him wance?

Bridgie One for the maid ...

Mikey A sow, a sow –

Bridgie An' one for the laddy-boy lives down the
lane.

Mikey A sow, they used te say, wudden't be safe
passin' his door.

SCENE FIVE

Carry transition by lighting change and by the intrusion of the wind. It works its way to a manic din. The curtains heave and snap in response. The wind exhausts itself. **Bridgie** *is unaffected.* **Mikey** *is perturbed. The wind's assault has impelled him to distraught movements about the space.*

Mikey (*babbling as he roams the space*) What I has te say is this, Bridgie, an' it's God's truth far as I can talk concernin' lifetimes ago only never was it at annie stage proposed be me that you were annie other nor the person ye were before God an' the world me lawful wedded that's te commence an' another sworn truth yes in said instance could be I was te blame which I no longer dispute for not clearin' the premises – curse o' God on me – not clearin' the whole pack o' them out ov it, if te be blemt for that so be it I shed salt tears for it every day o' me life since, I shudda swept the house o' them, din't I say it te the judge above on the bench for all the heed he tuk, a rabble chantin' o' cures an' incantayshuns nuthin' in them but out te harm the both of us an' me without a wink for a week the father pickin' that hour te die on top of all else I believe I tuk a turn I lost track of event lost sight o' rayson a serpent stray sod tuk me I luk'd up an' all gone everythin' we had the two of us was gone melted never te be no more ... (*Beat.*) An' that's what Mikey Cleary has te tell ye far as our calamtee is concerned.

Bridgie (*calm, seated, she has the pinafore plus needle and thread and appears to be fashioning a letter*) Je hear th'antics o' that gale? The Noise o' Time, I calls it. An'

Eternity? What about *it*? Me oul frien' the heron,
'nother great messenger-bird, tells me it's a *circle* – rim,
rim o' the circle (*gestures*) *everywhere*, if ye don' mind
now, and the centre (*another supporting gesture*)
nowhere. Say that over again, sez I, but he'd never, not
a bit of him, repayte it for me. (*Beat.*) Circle. Rim
(*gesturing*) *everywhere*. Centre (*reprising gesture*)
nowhere.

Mikey *looks at her, patiently bemused. He rises and
wanders.*

Bridgie He's thinkin' now the wrinkled dusk here is
beginnin' te affect damsel Bridgie.

Mikey *goes to the Singer and sits at it. He gets it going
uncertainly, and displays a tradesman's interest in its
workings.*

Mikey I remember the day the Singer was brought te
the house. Meself an' yer father took it from the cart
an' carried it in te the room for ye. Near let it fall goin'
from the kitchen te the room.

The sound of the heron comes intimately close. **Bridgie**
*listens. Something in her listening suggests collusion with
the heron, the heron's cry.* **Mikey** *looks excluded, threat-
ened. The heron's cry fades and is gone.*

Bridgie D'ye mind them herons used land near The
Pond in The Bare Field? Grey o' them wheelin' down
to the edge of the pond. Silvery grey. No, more bluey
grey. Slatey grey. Depind maybe on the light a particlar
hour, light'd alter the colour.

Mikey *nods vaguely.*

Bridgie I think (*nodding once*) that fella might be one o' them herons. Only a figayrie I have. Still ...

Mikey About what happened, Bridgie. Did ye hear what I was tryin' to tell ye there about what happened?

Bridgie *is on patrol.*

Bridgie 'Hag o' the air or homeless fairy?/Or were you spouse to a Mikey Cleary?/No, nay, never a witch, never fairy/Was once wedded to a man called Cleary.' Sit over there, Mikey –

She motions him to what has become his customary chair, downstage right. He leaves the Singer with a tickle of unease, and obeys.

Bridgie I've an inclinin', te look, te study, commotion.

She finds a chair and takes it with her. She sits, directly facing **Mikey**.

Bridgie Ye don't mind?

He nods assent, without conviction. Seated directly in front of him, she examines him, eyes first on his stockinged feet, working her way up to his tightly closed hands that are resting on his lap.

Bridgie Open the hands, Mikey. Show me them hands. I won't grab them an' make off with them – don't be afeared.

He opens his hands. Her gaze fixes on the blotched, upward palms.

Bridgie That's a bad vistayshun, qewman palm ever a delicate zone.

He closes his hands.

Bridgie No, Mikey, no – the way they were, layve them, layve them open.

Mikey *slugglishly obliges.* **Bridgie**, *at leisure, views the injured palms.*

Bridgie A load te carry. Show me the fists now, would ye.

Pause.

Bridgie Je hear me, Mikey?

He rises abruptly, almost leaves the space.

Bridgie Sit down, Mikey. It's all right. Don't vex yerself.

He sits, restless, with folded arms and head bowed, as if resisting a mug-shot. She rises, wanders to the Singer, leans against it and views him from that angle.

Bridgie Lift yer head, Mikey Cleary –

No response.

Bridgie Lift yer bothered head, will ye now?

Mikey (*head turned away*) Annie time I've a wish to converse, yer a wall. Now when it suits yer own minish-trayshuns, yer clawin' at me for te be an exhibit, is it? *Is it, Bridgie?* Why're ye clawin' at me for te be an exhibit?

Bridgie It's all right so.

Mikey *lifts his head and looks directly at her, 'permission' somewhere in the look. Pause.* **Bridgie** *moves towards him again. She sits beside him as before and resumes her inspection. She takes in his fists on his lap, and her gaze travels slowly up to his chest, his face, and rests there. Her eyes move from his jaw to his mouth, mouth to nose, to eyes, to forehead. That done, she rises slowly and circles him at a remove of a metre or so, viewing the head from various angles. Next, she takes the chair away, and sits.*

Mikey I was never as scrutineered since the day I entered the wastes o' Canada. Damn wonder ye didn't ask me to strip.

Bridgie Thank you, Mikey Cleary.

She takes to picking the imaginary fluff from her skirt. The space is more relaxed, has more breathing room now. **Bridgie** *resumes the needlework on the pinafore.* **Mikey**, *leisurely to the point where his rhythms become event, goes through his ointment routine, as though his wounded palms are all he has in the world.* **Bridgie** *cocks an ear; there is the lonesome bawl of an ass.* **Mikey** *eyes the pinafore.*

Mikey What'd y'ever see in that three-faced whipster Simpson?

Bridgie Shure didn't ye have great time for him yerself?

Mikey I let on te, outa pity, but I got the run of him quick enough. A man under boycott, no one do a hand's turn for him, an' it playzed you te do his messages – lug groceries te him, dainties an' whiskey an' the divil knows what.

Bridgie *continues with her needlework. Now she begins to stroll, and takes on touches of sensual energy.*

Bridgie (*almost teasing*) A man in distress, Mikey Cleary. There's the maiden in distress – world knows, knows well, her count'nance – but lots do forget there's also the man in distress. So. There's William Simpson, in his distress, public distress – not te menchin the sourpuss wife floggin' her crowshay: Hesther Simpson of the veiled demeanour – an' the two grand little lassies doin' their best te grow body an' soul in an undeservin' climate. Why wouldn't Bridgie Cleary offer the comether to a presentable idler the like o' William Simpson?

Mikey A grabber. An' a canat. An' the paycock strut, the *gatch* of him. The tweed, d'ye mind, an' the spats on the brogues for special doohs.

Bridgie Animals is great judges, y'know. My cat now had great time for William. An' th'oul collie dog too for that matter. Animals'll tell ye if there's something wrong with a body. It's them that knows.

Mikey I knew the smell o' him. Calm day or blowin' a gale, I'd know it yet.

Bridgie *is still mobile. Energised, she fondles the pinafore, scrutinises it with a certain tenderness, though a tickle of mischief is also evident.*

Bridgie How'd a body spell 'Susannah'? Ye'd think I never went te school – nor met even the scholars comin' home. Is that two *n*'s – 'Susannah'?

Mikey One o' them lavender kid-glove gintlemen. The whiff of him. Got it on you often enough.

Bridgie Two – I do believe. That young lassie was the spit of him. Them gawpy eyes. And bit of the lantern in the cut of the jaw, like all dug with th'other fut. Smell of him, is it? So? We spent time in bed – or snatched a rummagin' wherever fitted. Like lots, he was, God knows, often in a bit of a hurry, but I wasn't gernin'. A thing I remember – ye'd never guess it in his nature – but he'd breasts like a woman. (*Pause*) William Simpson. Landlord's Agent. Protestant Half-Gentry. 'Would ye back a gate, Bridgie?' Used tell him he had gran' breasts.

Mikey Wanted a chile by him, that be it, an' pass it off as ours, that on yer mind, Bridgie?

Long pause. **Bridgie** *is still strolling, but not as a prisoner; she could be strolling in a summer orchard. She stops at intervals to negotiate some challenge in the needlework.*

Bridgie God bless yer uproar, an' will ye listen te the truth of it? William Simpson – as compared to Phildy Reddan, me Egg-Man dear an' darlin'? In all dacency I have te state, in that two-horse point-to-point, Phildy

42

Reddan wins pullin' up, poor William o' the simple
virtues left at the start an' the mist descendin'.

Mikey (*as if he hasn't heard*)   Wanted a chile be
Simpson, an' pass the runt off as ours, that on yer
mind, Bridgie?

Bridgie   Chile be him? He wanted t'impregnate. He
wanted that. But. There's women has great bother
havin' a chile if they're not in the right disposition
towards the man, all knows that – an' Mikey Cleary
surely knows it too. William Simpson I didn't want for
the father of a chile o' my bearin'. We were never *that*
close. Locked limbs is one thing. Close is another.

Long pause. **Mikey** *has his back to the proceedings. He
looks 'out there' at a flap of the curtains.*

Mikey   He was false as water, me bucko, an' proved it
after, as is well known, showin' newsmen the tracks an'
the stains of other peoples' misfortunes, an' couldn't
have luk, an' didn't. The wife ailin' always – 'Her
Indoors!' Don't know what bekem o' the unfortunate
childer.

Mikey *holds to his 'abstensionist' position.* **Bridgie**'s *wanderings have taken her to a point directly behind* **Mikey**'s
*chair. She rests her hands on the back of the chair, but
without any hint of intimacy. At a certain point in the
speech below, she will resume her promenade, transforming
as she does to a woman joyously carrying a child.*

Bridgie   Still an' all, I did imagine a chile, an' greatly
regret it wasn't for te be – glory be to God, amn't I –

43

wasn't I – flesh-an'-blood, with flesh-an'-blood longin's?
I seen women up an' down the road, in wedlock an'
outa, seen them swell with the scantlin' 'ithin, rise with
milk o' the breasts, rise like barm. Often an' often I
watched them, roar inside me for that awakenin'. Hour
come, splash o' the waters, scantlin' out an' inta the
world. Feed then, rear, best ye can. Follies me yet.
Times mopin' here, I catch the squeal of a chile mighta
been mine. That's a true fact, Mikey Cleary. That's a
true fact.

Scene Six

Lighting change carries transition. **Bridgie** *is at the Singer. Her mood has altered again: she is back to her divilment side. Leaning back from the Singer, addressing it, she finger-motions – one, two, three – and makes lip movements in support. She repeats the routine.* **Mikey**, *who had been compulsively sharpening the teeth of a saw, has now noticed her activity.* **Bridgie** *repeats the routine for the third time. She is delighted as the Singer whirrs into independent life and enjoys a healthy gallop, then with graduated speed subsides.*

Bridgie (*provocatively*) Ye wouldn't believe how long it took me to get on spakin' terms with (*she fondles the Singer*) me ould segotia here.

Mikey (*to himself*) The Wandrin' Jew – that flung the boot at Christ – condemned from that day te wander roads o' the world.

Bridgie It took a Purgatory o' patience – a Singer can be terrible touch-me-not – but I kep' pettin' it until, with the dint o' coaxelorum, it gev in. Now we're great friends!

Mikey Could I ask ye somethin', Bridgie?

Bridgie No harm in askin' – ask away, Mikey Cleary.

Pause.

Mikey I was thinkin' *are* you Bridgie? (*Pause.*) Is it you – my Bridgie – that's in it?

Long pause.

Bridgie Say that again, would ye?

Mikey I'm askin' – *are* you Bridgie? Is it you – my Bridgie – that's in it?

Bridgie That was always yer question, wasn't it? Ever think of askin', 'Is it Mikey that's in it?'

Mikey Yer eludin' me question.

Bridgie The bother was I never cracked ye. Maybe I shudda tried harder, maybe I shudda gone about it some other way, maybe Mikey Cleary wasn't ever destined for the meetin' o' moment with Bridgie Cleary.

Mikey I'm askin': 'Is it you, my Bridgie, that's in it this minute?'

Pause. **Bridgie** *takes two attractive earrings from a pocket, puts them on, and looks at him. The light narrows to a spot on* **Bridgie** *to show how beautiful she is. The light opens to normal.*

Bridgie Never saw that woman before, I s'pose?

Mikey Glory be te Jayzus –

Bridgie Ever see her before?

Mikey Ne're saw the likes of her for beauty, tell ye that much.

Bridgie An' ye knew me mother, didn't ye? Did y'ever, did y'ever see this before on yer travels – have a look now. A good long gulp of a gawk.

Bridgie *rises and comes to centre-stage position. Pause. She goes perfectly still. He's watching, intent. Her hands are resting easily by her upper thighs. With a quick, graceful movement her hands are extending before her at waist height, palms up. She holds them there for the count of five. With another quick movement her hands swivel, her palms now pointing downward for the count of five.* **Bridgie** *relaxes.*

Bridgie The mother's jiggle-o'-the-hands used to give ye a stannin' wakeness, if I remember rightly.

Mikey Mothers! My mother wouldn't give me the time o' day.

Bridgie Ye were hard done by, were ye, hind-tit only, that it?

Mikey She damn near med an orphan o' me. At layst your mother'd give me a cup o' tay.

Bridgie The mother an' me used have the odd right spat too, have te be dug outa each other. But I'll tell ye wan thing, if she was alive that night I'd ha' been minded.

Mikey (*rush of speech, barely intelligible*) That crab outa hell, Dunne, prancin' the floor an' breedin' lunacies lek he was fresh ruz up from the sewers o' perfidy ... I'd take back the whole thing if I cud, we'd all take back lots if we cud, but there's things can't be tuk back, nuthin' te be dun.

Bridgie *is not interested.*

Bridgie An' d'ye remember the mother's folly-up jiggle-o'-the-hands? Do ye?

Mikey *watches, curious and fearful.*

Bridgie We'll do the two together, cos it's good for you, and good for me, they be given a reglar airin'. Matter o' fack, I used often try them out on me own here – damn sight more to them nor quackery, I'll warrant ye.

Expertly, with tremendous grace, **Bridgie** *gives a reprise of the first hand-dance.*

Bridgie An' here's the folly-up one, if I have it right.

Her hands, to commence, are resting easily by her sides. She raises her right hand toward her left shoulder and lets it float there, index finger extended. Beat. She moves her left hand, index finger extended, across her body, the finger pointing downward to a spot just right of her foot. She holds for the count of five. She breaks from the pose.

Bridgie Ye recall how that used quiet the *ree-raw* an' the *roolye-boolye*?

Mikey Well I mind, well I mind ...

Bridgie *sits and passes the time playing with a spool of blue thread.*

Mikey Y'are. Y'are my Bridgie. I'm sorry. Doan hould

it agin me. I do get cracked notions, couldn't tell ye
from the Pope's tooth where they come from, only I'd
be glad te get rid o' them once an' for all. That I
would. I searched the streets of Montreal, Bridgie, I
pounded them cobbles lukin' for my wife Bridgie
Cleary. The place was full of Irish – men, women, an'
childer. I stopped in me tracks a hundred times an'
wheeled an' chased – hidin' from the traffic as best I
could – ran after a woman just gone past an' she the
spit o' you, whip through the rush of people – men
snappin' at me – catch up, an' luk, an' find meself
lukin' inta a freckened face the lek o' yours: hair the
same, cheek-bones, lie o' the face, eyes, only it's not me
wife Bridgie Cleary, it's a freckened face an' a shout for
help formin'. I dun that again an' again until I had te
curb the rush of it or it'd have finished me. So, havin'
te curb it, I larn'd te choke it.

*He sets off around the space, ominously slow now, and with
his head obsessively bowed. This movement brings him to a
halt upstage of* **Bridgie**. *He focuses on her, targets her. He
walks slowly towards her, looks discoveringly at her.
Recognition, relief suffuses him. He extends a hand to touch
her, but he doesn't dare.*

Mikey You're Bridgie. You're my Bridgie. Y'always
was my Bridgie. I shudda bin struck dead for what I let
happen.

Pause. **Bridgie** *is seated by the table.* **Mikey** *takes a chair
and joins her.*

Mikey Or with a woman, in a shebeen or a bed,
they'd always say: 'Yer not talkin' te me, Mikey Cleary,

yer talkin' te another woman, don't ye know a woman can always tell when a man's not talkin' te her but talkin' te a woman not present who houlds the command, so would ye talk te me direck, Mikey Cleary, have the dacency te tell us yer woman-story cos if ye don't tell it te someone an' keep tellin' until yer fever abates, ye'll drive all qewman company from ye, animals too likely, an' invite fracture an' be taken away an' no more about ye.'

Mikey *takes off his cap, tugs at it, examines it as if studying his own disturbed skull. He sits it on his right hand, extends the arm, and stares at the cap. He stops.*

Mikey (*same compelled vein*)   An' I mind one St Patrick's Night in Montreal, Canada, an' I'm sittin' sippin' whisky with another woman, it was always another becos how'd annie wan woman be attindin' to a ramblin' amadhaun, once'd be more nor sufficient te sicken a body, an' this woman is lisnin' – pity in her, I could tell that, an' pity is poison te take but a man'll take pity if there's no more te be had, an' I'm talkin' oskewrly as usual ov a woman other than the woman I'm with, I'm spakin' indireck of me wife departed, an' the woman says, 'Mikey' – an' I stopped. She says, 'Is there a warp in you?' 'What d'ye mayne?' says I. Says she, 'Some warp – is there in you the warp o' jealousy?' 'Yer rayson for askin'?' 'Only a question,' says she, lukin through me an out t'other side. 'It shivers the tree, Mikey,' says she. 'Envy, spite, jealousy, madnesses o' that nature shivers the tree,' says she, 'but jealousy in special is the ruin o' many.' An' she tuk a hanky from her pocket – all aroun' watchin', lek we were on a painted stage – tuk this hanky, leans over, an' wipes a mizzle o' sweat from offa me forehead. 'Mind yerself, Mikey,' says she, an' she left.

Mikey *takes out the ointment box, places it between them. He extends his afflicted palms and looks at them. There's an ambiguous invitation in the movement.* **Bridgie** *studies him, but he won't meet her gaze. She takes up the box, opens it, looks at the contents, sniffs the contents, and leaves the lid and the box on the table. She looks at him again. This time he takes her gaze, after his fashion.*

Bridgie   Tuk ye a while te talk lek that, Mikey Cleary.

Mikey   I was never gifted the gab, Bridgie, all knows that.

Bridgie   While for you te talk, while for me te listen ...

Mikey   At the latter end, there's only two sounds in the world –

Bridgie   An' what's them, tell us?

Mikey   The scythe singin' ripe is the meado', an' the scythe hittin' stone.

Bridgie (*nods*)   Who toul' ye that now, Mikey Cleary?

He looks at her but says nothing.

Bridgie (*kindly*)   Musta learned that among th'ointmen'-haired Red Injuns an' the Mounties or in yer long warehouse nights on the wharves o' Montreal. What ye larn on yer travels is the only gold ye'll ever know, it's true. At thirteen the mother told me, 'Look, chile, for yer *Ninth Wave of the Sea.*'

Mikey Wave? *Ninth Wave?*

Bridgie Carries the treasure, Mikey – ye didn't hear that on yer rambles? At eighteen I gev meself to a made match. An' that was all right. An' then it wasn't. I tuk a lover. An' shure that was grand. Then somethin' else happened. What happened was what y'always wait for te happen. I fell in love with a purty man. Dangerous man besides – no complaints about that. Love's a fire, and fire's a danger – learn that for yer *ABC*, tell it to yer childer in time te be. I fell, I fell, I fell in love with a purty man. An' that cudda been, that cudda been Bridgie Cleary's *Ninth Wave of the Sea* ...

Pause.

Mikey We've a visitor, Bridgie. An' oul' friend.

Bridgie *follows* **Mikey's** *gaze upstage.* **William Simpson** *has arrived.*

Mikey Knew he'd turn up, me bucko. I'd a sworn it –

Bridgie William. William Simpson. (*Beat.*) *Fáilte*, William Simpson, *fáilte* ...

William *is a plump, fresh-looking fifty-plus, fresh with the caveat that he shares the sepia pallor that goes with this territory. He's well dressed, verging on the fancy dresser. He sports a cutaway collar, spats, and a moustache.*

William   Bridgie – there you are. And, it's you, Mikey, isn't it? Greatly changed, not greatly changed ... I'm glad to see you, Bridgie. And Mikey, how are you keeping? (*Beat.*) Excuse me one moment –

Shamelessly, he takes a mirror from his pocket and finds, somehow, a place to hang it. He busies himself combing his hair, his moustache, fixing his collar. In the middle of these antics he half-stops and gestures to **Bridgie** *and* **Mikey.**

William   Just one second, and I'll be right as a trivet –

Mikey (*snarling*)   An' sweet as a nut, an' game as a gander.

William *resumes his titivations and completes the job in his own leisurely time.* **Mikey** *and* **Bridgie** *simply watch,* **Bridgie** *idling with the spool of blue thread, but she's thoroughly alert to this new scenario, this developing action.* **Mikey** *is keeping his attention, happily, on the antics of the industrious* **William.**

Mikey (*commenting*)   Our Father who art in heav'n halla'd be Thy Name! Holy Mary Mother o' God pray for us sinners now an' at the hour of our death. *Amin* maynes *So Be It*!

William   Good! That's much better!

He turns from the mirror.

Bridgie (*slyly*)   That was gran', William Simpson.

William   It was, Bridgie?

Bridgie   Ye'd pay to watch it.

William (*to the world*)   Bridgie still sees me as –

Bridgie   'Popinjay!'

Mikey   I wouldn't –

William   Wouldn't what, Cleary?

Mikey   *Cleary!* Pay te watch it, *Simpson.*

William   No? (*He takes the offensive, his tone not far from patronising.*) The bit of style, applied with the bit of style. Poor world without the bit o' style, don't ye think?

Mikey, *in a stew of resentments, rises and slowly advances on* **William**. *Both are standing as they confront each other.* **Bridgie** *is an interested spectator.*

Mikey (*examining* **William**)   Same ould Simpson …

William   Same ould Cleary, come to that.

Bridgie (*to the audience*)   *Different* Bridgie!

William *studies her.*

William   Yes, that's true, I think that's true.

Bridgie (*half-jokingly*)   A middlin' scholar only, but I do be at me lessons. Every ding-dong day! No days here, but shure what matter? (*Merrily.*) I often thought,

'Days o' the week, roun' an' roun', ye'd get tired o' them aisy enough.'

Mikey I jus wanta throw an eye over ye, William Simpson.

William If that's what pleases you, Mikey, why not? It's been quite some time, hasn't it?

Bridgie (*to anyone*) 'The men squarin' up t'other' – Glory be to God! *A Nation Once Again!*

Mikey *insolently extends a hand to* **William***'s chin, settles the disposition of the face to his satisfaction, looks long into* **William***. Then, with equal insolence, he shifts the face once to the left, once to the right, so that he can digest each profile.*

William Is this an identification parade?

Mikey It's an inspeckshin.

William Make it quick, Mikey.

Bridgie Will ye not ask him te sit down itself, Mikey Cleary?

Mikey O, ekskews me! I forgot me manners. (*He gets a chair, places it.*) Sit down there, William Simpson, Esquire. Rest yer larded bones.

William *sits. The Singer whirrs into exuberant life, does its number.* **William** *watches, listens with the air of a confused traveller. The Singer coasts to quiet.*

Mikey (*old lag*) Now d'ye mind, William Simpson!
Quick larnin' here for slow beginners!

Bridgie, *smiling, nods a greeting to the Singer.*

Mikey But shure we'll help ye along the best we can –
as we always dun, I seems te remember.

William (*placatory, and yet not*) You're not changed,
Mikey, but you are greatly aged, I'd say.

Mikey Shut yer face a minit, will ye, Simpson.
Esquire. Mikey Cleary's just runnin' his ruler across a
play-actor he thought he knew, a while back ...

Mikey *focuses on the spats in a kind of delight. He looks
silently, gleefully towards* **Bridgie** *and (gesturally) draws
her attention to the spats, which, it follows, begin to glow.*

Mikey If ye had te turn up, Simpson, Esquire, I'd a
laid a wager ye'd land here airin' them spats. (*Pause.*)
We used say ye slithered inta the world wearin' spats –
a rare class ov a deliv'ry – only to be found now an'
agin among the half-gintry.

William Will this take long, Mikey?

Mikey Why? Are ye in a hurry?

Bridgie Get it over, Mikey Cleary.

Mikey Never fret, it won't take long. I'm raysonable
familiar with the speciment before me. (*Another
insolent general inspection.*) Ye minded yerself well,

Simpson, Esquire. Or ye were well minded. Or the two o' them things, that'd be te be it, more likely. (*He glances at* **Bridgie**.) Divil the much changes. A bit too sweet to be wholesome. Does anniethin' change? Divil the much.

Mikey *drops his investigation and shifts to a downstage position, where he sits, broody. Clearly an outburst will not be long delayed. As action involving* **William** *and* **Bridgie** *develops,* **Mikey** *sinks dangerously into himself. He comes out of it, then gives himself to putting on his boots, lacing them up with wicked intent.*

Meanwhile, **William** *takes off his coat, puts it carefully aside, and looks at his spats – will he, won't he? Next, he moves about, checking the scene, glancing 'out', half-acknowledging* **Bridgie**, *who is speaking, half to herself.*

Bridgie (*as though in a reverie*)   Now we'll hear all the newses from Ballyvadlea – births, deaths, marriages, childer an' by-childer, the price of eggs, turkeys, hins, guinea-hins, what the priest roared outa him last Sunda, various unrests, another landlord shot, a bullock maimed, who won the hurlin' at Mullinahone, who was stretched an' who The Hayro, an' who put the bad eye on them geese in the meado' other side o' the watercressy strayme there ...

William, *arriving at the Singer, gives his attention to* **Bridgie**, *who is downstage from him.*

William   Bridgie Cleary made –

Bridgie   Weskits for the gentry, hats for the quality –

William You had such a gift in those hands, Bridgie, nothing you couldn't put together in no time. Well, it was recognised, wasn't it?

Bridgie Wait till I show ye –

Bridgie *moves to the drawer of the Singer and produces the pinafore.*

Bridgie One of the pieces I do be at, for Susannah. See – the letterin' there – how's Susannah, tell us?

William Married a fool, living in Cork.

Bridgie An' Denise?

William Married an invalid. Marooned in Kanturk.

Bridgie And Hesther, crowshayin' away –

William You know Hesther – Hesther's 'grand' – poor old Hesther. She was never in her health, really ...

The anguished bawl of an ass intrudes. **William** *stirs uneasily.*

William There's a sound I could never stand, not from the first day it assaulted me.

Bridgie (*teasing*) Wouldn't ye not pity a jack-ass, William, all that sap in their haunches an' what in God's name is they goin' to do with it an' spring dancin' over the hill ...

William *won't pursue this theme.*

William (*to* **Bridgie**)   What, what's it like – in this place? What goes on? (*Beat.*) Does anything – *happen*?

Mikey   What goes on? Does anniethin' happen? Before we dayle with them enquiries, would you tell me wan thing, Mr William Simpson, Esquire?

William   Certainly, if it's in my power. What is it you wish to know, Mikey?

Mikey   I wish te know what entered you – what ruz inside ye, an' tuk y'over from yer thrapple to the balls of yer big toes, that you, Simpson, William, s'posed frien' o' Mikey Cleary an' reglar consoler atween the sheets of his wife Bridgie – what atween us an' all harrum tuk universal possession of Honorable William Simpson to th'extint that – Bridgie Cleary swep from the world an' her husban' Mikey Cleary bound for jail on trumpery charges, said Simpson, Esquire, could find his way to gainful employment guidin' an' directin' snooper newsmen, cameras unner their oxters, guidin' them an' other stray visitors from the four tainted quarters, steerin' an' organisin' processions of same, in an' out of the dwellin'-house of couple aforementioned, not to spake of draggin' throngs across the few acres adjoinin' te point out further special attractions, satisfy the curiosity buds of all comers, supply te their bellies' contint recipes of scannal an' calamtee till they'd spew gold, silver an' gold for Lavender Kid-Glove Simpson, Master o' Ceremonies, an' Much Obliged, half-a-sovrin's gran', tell people I'm here, mind yerself now on the road home.

William *plays with his moustache anxiously.*

Bridgie (*only remotely engaged*)   That's a long mouthful. A lot o' words, Mikey Cleary, a lotta words there ...

William   I did have the key to the house – yes – if that's what you mean.

Mikey   No bother to ye –

William   Because you asked me – you may remember – to look after the dog.

Bridgie (*to audience*)   Ranger – the collie – I remember Ranger. An' d'yiz remember me darlin' cat, Dotey – what became o' *her*?

Mikey   I asked ye to luk after the dog. I had to be deminted not te unnerstan' that somethin' in you wouldn't skip the chance – once the grabber always the grabber – wouldn't skip the chance te velvet yer greedy-gut pockets with the divdens of others' misfortunes, an' not contint with that, I was brought the tidin's in me prison cell! Got so fond o' the key te the dwellin'-house o' Mikey Cleary an' his wife departed, so fond they had to put the law on ye in the long latter end te recover our key and regain possession of the premises from Simpson, Esquire, of the trained moustache, an' the curry-combed spats an' the ramblin' fingers itchy for the rumps o' the lonesome ladies.

Pause. **William** *seeks a foothold in* **Bridgie**'s *territory.*

William   The pinafore, Bridgie ... Susannah often spoke of you, y'know. She'd great time for you – great time for you, Bridgie – always ...

Mikey   Simpson Esquire has nuthin' te say te the charges livelled!

Bridgie (*toying with the pinafore*)   I'd a *grá* for that child. Used think she knew, William ...

Mikey   Free with the tongue as a gineral rule – but nuthin' te say te the charges livelled!

William   Knew?

Mikey   He'll sing tho', before I'm through with him.

William   How 'knew', Bridgie?

Bridgie   About us – y'know ...

Mikey   By Christ, he'll lay truth on the board consarnin' his betrayals 'gin them that minded him an' the hard day in it.

Bridgie   The way childer'll pick up what's goin'on ... I believe she knew all right, that chile, the time the pair of us were whilin' the time. There's childer in it has more in their heads nor their nimble prayers. (*Pause.*) Kem to me wan day that chile did – Susannah, she'd mek ye melt in yer stannin' – kem to me this day, an' sez she, 'Bridgie, Bridgie, Bridgie Cleary, bathe me with tears, Bridgie, dry me with kisses ...' (*Beat.*)

61

Couldn't ever forget that, from them lips, lips of a chile, 'Bathe me with tears, Bridgie, then dry me, dry me with kisses-o ...'

Scene Seven

Lighting changes to carry transition. **Mikey** *is compulsively untying and tying his bootlaces.* **William** *is brushing his spats with a wire brush.* **Bridgie** *is patiently performing her twisting-finger-in-ear routine.*

Mikey Quare thing but I never even liked the curse-o'-God cooperin'. Not a stitch on ye but'd carry the smell o' some dip or dye an' timber trayted with rubs an' soaks tormentin' te breathe an' battrin' metal hoops that'd fight ye lek their lives hinged on bestin' ye an' the day-long hurlamabock of it'd twist yer arse gut Christ sweet Christ on the rocks o' Calvary I often said – arrah, there's no good talkin' about it, great weather for young ducks.

William You kept it up, Mikey, the cooperin'?

Mikey Didn't I have te give it over, years back – some disayse on me hands ...

William On your hands?

Mikey That's what I said.

William (*coolly*) Doesn't surprise me, now you confess it. May even have heard the story somewhere on my travels.

Mikey Yer own paws spotless, I s'pose?

Bridgie *comes to life in an automaton vein.*

Bridgie Are you a witch or are you a fairy/Or are you the wife of Mikey Cleary?/I was never a witch, never a fairy/Was once married to a man called Cleary ...

Mikey Don't start that now, Bridgie, like a dacent lassie –

William Leave her be, will you?

Bridgie Sometime fresh, more often weary/I sought a lover would treat me fairly/Step forward, William, shoulders squarely/An' show yer a match for Bridgie Cleary ...

William Go on, Bridgie, go on.

Mikey Ye whelp ye, can't ye see she's distressin' herself?

William That what you call it?

Mikey Wait till yev all her ramblin's off be heart.

Bridgie (*in the same vein*) Forward, William, shoulders squarely/Show yer a match for Bridgie Cleary ...

Mikey Bridgie –

William The one wise move I ever made, taking up that offer ...

Mikey Not that many ye refused, be all accounts.

Bridgie, *the shirt in her possession, calmly tears it to pieces. She wanders the space, leaving a piece here and a piece there, making a thing of the choice of location for these relics. She could almost be putting up branches of holly or palm.*

Bridgie (*matter-of-factly*) What's a made match? An aisy question te start the class. What is a made match? Mikey?

Mikey Made match is what works, if ye makes it yer business te see that it works – jus lek lots o' things. An' if ye don't mek it yer business te see that it works, then the wheels fly off an' there's nuthin' but *tranglam* an' *weelya-wailye*. That's my defnishin.

Bridgie William – you – what's a made match, tell us?

William Well, made match – custom of the people, Bridgie – foolish custom, hucksterin', the best of times, low-class auction ...

Bridgie The votes is comin' in – thank-ye kindly, sir, she said. I've heard it proclaimed, 'Every match is a made match, only some made in heaven, some not.' That's only confusin' matters is Bridgie Cleary's verdick – that's goin' outa the smoke an' inta the smother. What I'd say is, 'Let the match-makers banished be – cos it won't come right.'

William Bravo, Bridgie! More power to you, more power.

Mikey (*with divilment*) Was you an' Hesther a made match, Simpson?

William I beg your pardon –

Bridgie (*placing her remaining bits of the dismembered shirt on* **William** *and* **Mikey** *in turn*) You see, there's this preshis matter o' choosin' freely. An' in your prechis time o' choosin' – here's somethin' I'd tell te all the childer I never had – in the hour o' choosin' ye must keep yer eyes open.

Mikey Shure isn't that the bother – for young an' ould?

Bridgie Hould them open. Might help ye, mightn't be no help at all – we're given te blunders, y'see.

William World's made of blunders, I believe ...

Mikey Aye, an' boulders. Mostly boulders.

Bridgie So, sooner or later, ye'd better find the bird in the tree – messenger-bird, an' that's the bird'll tell ye, truth o' yer nature, yer longin'.

Mikey (*to audience*) That has te be wan wise bird!

William Truth of your longing ...

Bridgie Yer at the tree, there's the bird, an' the bird'll advise. But now, Mikey Cleary, now, William Simpson, question is, 'Will you go with what yer tould, will ye go with the truth – truth o' yer road, yer nature?'

Mikey 'Hell is failin' te find the track o' yer road.' Blacksmith tould me that. Preacher blacksmith, puss on him as long as a midnight shada.

William And the tree – messenger-bird there – what were you advised, Bridgie?

Bridgie (*she hasn't heard a word of him*) Go with the truth or stay with dittherum-dattherum – there's lots quake at that lep!

She skips on to a chair and looks down as if she were on the brow of a cliff. The heron sound passes. She listens, then returns to her theme.

Bridgie O, yes, mek no mistake, lots quake, an' the quake can undo. Maynin'? Maynin' there's a moment, *a gamble moment –*

She sways on the perch of the chair, jumps to the floor, and steadies.

Bridgie A moment there is an' ever will be/ *Chuala mé an scéal ó mo Leannán Luí* ... An' for sweeteners – *Won't come twice, Bridgie, from over the sea ...*

She sits and goes quite still. She has gone into herself, diving into her own reflection as she described in Scene One. The two men study her, uncertain of the next move.

Mikey Bridgie, Bridgie, Bridgie Cleary – how'd ye keep up with her?

William Do you ever listen to her, Mikey?

Mikey   She gets botherations. Did ye meet her at all, ye *glibeen* ye, an' you an' her whilin' the time? Then agin, love is blind is an ould sayin'. *Love is blin' an' lovers cannot see.* (*Pause.*) Love is blin' an' lovers cannot see ...

Pause.

William   What would you know about love?

Mikey   Skews me?

William   What would you know about love?

Mikey   What'd I know about love? What does anniewan know about love, William Simpson? For meself, only answer I can give ye is – nuthin'. I knows nuthin' about it beyond as follies: ye larn te breathe accorn' te the measure o' love ye lend te people, an' accorn te the bounty o' wan or two women ye meet on yer way. That's all Mikey Cleary can tell ye about it. If yev anniethin' te add te that, he'll be glad te hear it, William Simpson.

William *hesitates, momentarily humbled.*

William   What was it again?

Mikey   Skews me?

William   About love – what you said there –

Mikey   I said, 'A body larns te breathe accorn' te th'amount o' love given t'another – others – an' you steppin' the world.'

Pause.

William   Yes. Taking, yes, the chances you have of loving. That's what the heart's for, I suppose ...

Bridgie *comes to life again.*

Bridgie   I was away for a dip! Ready for the pair o' yiz now.

She takes the blue hanky from her pocket, eyes **William***, advances on him with the step of a prosecuting attorney. Her 'breather' has energised her.*

Bridgie   You put it about, didn't ye, you were in the process o' puttin' it about that this biteen of turqouisey blue – near-enough turqouisey – was a present for me bucko William, whereas well an' well ye knew it was for another – an' quite another – for, truth be told, a frien', bosom-te-bosom frien', one Phildy Reddan – Egg-Man Phildy – of whom, of whom, William Simpson, an' small blame, you were jealous as the cat!

William   I'm not the jealous type, Bridgie. Wouldn't waste time on –

Bridgie   As the cat! Jealousy at home, jealousy abroad, behold (*pointing to* **Mikey**) the man there said it – jealousy that shivers the timber! Di'nt ye say that, Mikey Cleary?

Pause. Focus turns to **Mikey**.

Mikey   What?

Bridgie Di'nt I hear ye say that, Mikey Cleary?

Mikey 'Bout jealousy?

Bridgie Correct!

Pause.

Mikey It's a canker. Th'original canker. Shivers whatever it meets.

Bridgie Shivers the timber, aye, an' splits the rock! An' it travels – gives th'orders – ye can't see it, an' yet, mind yerself!

Bridgie *is now playing with a reprise of her gestural score on the subject of eternity.*

Bridgie Rim everywhere, centre nowhere! That's the sweep an sway o' jealousy!

William I wasn't jealous. The Egg-Man – a dalliance. I knew I was loved. I had my lacks but I can tell when a woman loves me – just as I could tell when I loved the woman. You loved me, Bridgie. As I loved you. The whole parish knew it – and said it, to my face – and that for me was cause for celebration. I can honestly say I don't think I'd ever been in love till then – not like that certainly, not like that. Do you believe me, Bridgie? Bridgie? Were you listening to what I said there?

Mikey They say nuthin' strikes lek jealousy. Severs the roots.

Bridgie *hasn't heeded* **William**'s *claim. She focuses on the air, the bits of shirt still adorning the two men.*

Bridgie   O, (*suiting actions to the words*) I'll take back them samples now. I'd an urge te view them at a small remove – dress-maker habits die hard, ye see ... Day might come we'll have a reglar fittin' here – I used love the lie o' garments shapin' roundly te their destinations.

The heron cries again, those croaks, fading.

Bridgie   They say that under the full moon the herons do go inta a trance lukin' at their own shadas in the water. Others sez they're more ghosts nor birds. Heard a story once of a heron stole a man's cap, flew down, whipped it offa his head, dropped it in the next field. An' – wud ye believe it – came the week after an' whipped it offa the man's head again an' made off with it. Not the best o' signs, everywan said. The man ruz up an' fled for America – an' didn't the boat go down, a hundred drownded. Ye'd be afeared te go out the door.

Mikey   Ett a heron wance. Fish-taste'd rise yer gorge.

William   I knew I was loved. So why should I be jealous? I can tell you from that experience what I think love is – that was the time I found out – you don't forget that, y'know. Certain things can't ever be taken from you – that's what I mean – about love ...

Mikey   Of a sudden everyone's talkin' o' love! Never heard it mentioned, no, not wance, all me days in Ballyvadlea! Montreal neither.

Bridgie *is not listening. She is occupied playing with a movement score based on the heron wading, the heron on full alert, the heron pouncing to spear a fish, or a hat. The bias of the movement is towards the abstract.*

William   I told you, Bridgie, at the time, didn't I? I said, 'Love is the man dreaming, waking up, and he finds it true' – that's what I said, didn't I, Bridgie? Do you remember? I told you that –

Mikey   You were jealous, Simpson.

William   Was I?

Mikey   A catchin' disayse. Put ye in mind o' shingles, slaps a belt 'round ye, red raw killer belt, make bits o' ye.

Bridgie (*returning*)   You remember the herons?

William   And the heronry, Bridgie. Yes, I do, well I remember –

Bridgie   That's the word – I was tryin' te get a hould of it – that's the word ye had for the congregayshun o' them. Give it te me again.

William   A *heronry*.

Bridgie   A *heronry* ...

A far ripple of the piano scales touches **Mikey**'s *hearing.*

Bridgie   I – wait now – I hear a song comin'.

Mikey Rise it, Bridgie.

Bridgie I believe I'll sing a song.

William 'Slievenamon', Bridgie?

Mikey Give us the raw bar there.

Bridgie Song for an absent friend had a way of lisnin',
the match o' that lisnin' you'll meet very seldom on yer
bendy road. I shud be grateful, I met it a couple o'
times – maybe that's all is ever allowed us under the
tough ould stars. Two or three has the secret o' lisnin',
an' we shuddent ask fer more.

Pause. **Bridgie** *sings.*

Bridgie Alone, all alone, by the wave-washed
strand/All alone in a crowded hall/The hall it is gay an'
the waves they are grand/But my heart is not there at
all. (*Beat.*) It flies far away, by night an' by day/Te the
time an' the joys that are gone/An' I never can forget,
the sweet maiden I met/In the valley near
Slievenamon.

Extended pause.

William Slievenamon ...

Mikey Shure isn't that it?

William 'Mountain of the Women', I believe.

Bridgie Slievenamon.

SCENE EIGHT

Carry transition with lighting and a piano idling over the notes of 'Slievenamon'.

William *is standing stage left, looking at the floor with a dangerous immobility.* **Bridgie** *is seated centrally, counting silently with finger movement accompaniment.* **Mikey** *is sitting downstage left, abrasively* en garde, *sensing an assault is nigh. The space crackles with tension.*

William (*to audience*)   Something I must say out, and I must say it out now. It has to do with Cooper Cleary. Concerning him, I'm grateful for one particular thing. My last thought on earth was, 'Pray God, wherever I land, I'll have the chance to say certain words to Cooper Cleary, say into that hangdog face at last, for the good of my health –'

Mikey   An' you dead!

William   Tell him that one of the wretched spectacles of my life was Mikey Cleary. In a drench of jealousy that I saw gathering for years –

Mikey   I knew this'd come. Rise it, Squire!

William   Jealousy of Bridgie for the woman she was, jealousy of her pleasuring times with me, jealousy of her in the arms of the Egg-Man. The day came, it *had* to. The Cooper assembled his Hottentot thugs and near relations and locked and barred the cottage door and between paraffin oil and cross-eyed pishoguery and apeman savageries did away with a lovely woman.

74

On 'lovely woman' **Mikey** *rises and makes for* **William**.
Bridgie *rouses from her silent preoccupations, steps with
authority between the two, and parts them. She leads*
Mikey *back to his position, repositions his chair so that it is
now facing cross-stage, and puts him sitting there. That
done, she takes* **William** *and seats him in the corresponding
position, stage left. She settles herself upstage of the two, in
an assertive arbitrator role. The men wait. The pause is
extended to the maximum.* **Bridgie** *looks up, focuses on*
William, *and nods.* **William** *has leave to speak.*

William   Why did none of us stop him? We couldn't
believe – no one could – that he'd turn killer. Your
illness, Bridgie – that fever you took, and no wonder –
gave him his chance. Suddenly, it wasn't a fever, it was
something queer, it was something dangerous. It was a
changeling there in the bed, not Bridgie at all, and
what was needed now? Why, only one thing – get hold
of Witch-Doctor Jack Dunne.

Mikey   *Were you present, Scrimshanker?*

William   Dunne sang his charms and spells, worked
your mob to a frenzy, but it was you, Cooper, nobody
else but you, you lit the fire, fanned the blaze, doused
Bridgie with paraffin, burned her beautiful life away.

Mikey   *You were present?*

William   Why don't you fall on your knees and beg
her pardon, if you're a man at all? Murder can't be
undone but, at least, have the honesty to admit her
death on your hands. Might clear the air, give you –
give us all – some colour of ease ...

Bridgie (*to herself*) 'Don't go makin' a herring of her on that fire,' somebody said. 'Don't go makin' a herring o' Bridgie Cleary ...'

William Hottentots! Cave-Men! Troglodytes!

Mikey *Trogglewhat?*

William Disembowelling too good for the lot of you!

Mikey Watch what ye're sayin', Honorable Yer Honour, ye'll make a knot with yer tongue yer teeth might find hard te loosen. Repayte queschin – if I've layve t'open me mouth in this Kang'roo Court: were you a witness to the events yer takin' on te describe?

William There was no scarcity of witnesses.

Mikey D'ye tell me now? Glory be!

William Only their memories failed them – Patrick Pig and Michael Muck have a traditional weakness that way, I seem to recall.

Mikey But *you* wasn't a witness, Scrimshanker?

Bridgie *has started picking imaginary fluff from* **Mikey's** *clothing, gathering it into her palm and then, at intervals, blowing it off into the air.*

William Had I been, Cleary, what happened wouldn't have happened.

Mikey But yer Honour, Simpson *wasn't* a witness, an'

Mikey Cleary happens te know why, shure didn't the stray dogs o' the townland know it. You weren't a witness, becos on the night in queschin, poor Bridgie lyin' there in a whirl o' fever, brave William was too busy te call becos, led be his tool, he's off comfortin' another man's wife in the next parish, he must have his chew o' the tit!

William   Don't listen to this filth, Bridgie.

Bridgie *is now doing her 'picking fluff' routine on* **William***'s clothing.*

Mikey   He must have his shlurp o' the tit! *Sook-sook, sook-sook-sook* – he's in grief cos an Egg-Man is slipped atween him an' his reglar jollifications – so, on the night when he might ha' been a witness, he's otherwise occupied.

William   The reason I wasn't there on the evening you and your gang cut loose, as you well know, since it was mentioned in Court, was that Susannah was ill. The child was choking with a bad cough and I was looking for the doctor to come and see her – and, drunkard that he was, he couldn't be found.

Mikey   Mindin' a sick chile, moryah!

William   *Possessed – eaten out of it –* by jealousy!

Mikey   Devoted husban' an' father, moryah!

William   *You* were the one possessed, it was *you* needed attention –

Bridgie *raises a peremptory hand.*

Bridgie   Please to be quiet – I can't stir with the din.

She walks to the Singer, and sits, quiet in the space. Extend pause to the maximum. The quiet is banished by the intrusion of a mockery-tinted mélange of the gale, heron, piano scales, ass's roar. The racket commands the space for ten to fifteen seconds, then slowly whirls away out of hearing.

Bridgie   Susannah *was* poorly.

William   That's right, Bridgie. Susannah was poorly.

Mikey   A gran' story an' he tells it lovely!

Bridgie   Susannah was poorly because Bridgie was in peril – and that's gospel. I'd a bond to that chile. There was a way, some way or other (*fondling the pinafore*), that she was the chile I never had. Aye, an' she was the sister I never had. An' – ye could say – the woman-frien' I never had. The pair of us could talk without talkin' at all, that was the way of it. She'd know, always an' ever, she'd know if I was unwell or any way endangered. She'd know – an' bear the brunt, body an' soul. That was Susannah, as I knew her for te be.

Pause. **Bridgie** *resumes work on the pinafore.* **Mikey,** *seated, is trapped in the air.* **William** *patrols restlessly. The tension in the space is unrelieved.*

Mikey   I knows I shudda cleared that gathrin' – didn't I say it in Court?

No one gives heed.

William   Something I want you to know, Bridgie –
that talk you heard from your murdering husband of
my showing reporters about the house, and, worse,
taking money for so doing, and, on top of all, taking
possession of your cottage that lay there empty, that
was – is – vicious slander.

Bridgie *is not listening.*

Bridgie   Wasn't Susannah's first time on earth, believe
you me ...

Mikey (*to himself*)   Warp o' jealousy – is that you,
Mikey Cleary? Will someone tell me this: how does a
man know when he's in the grip of the lek o' that, how
does a body know when a body's possessed?

William   Someone had to step forward – someone
with authority – to keep the traffic under control. I did
that. The people, generally, were grateful I was there to
see to it. Someone had to do it.

Mikey   Lek I said te Bridgie, stand on a serpent stray
sod – how d'ye know the, the consequences of a thing
the lek o' that, entrin' ye, unbeknownst, an' spillin' ye
inta the mists of unrayson. Is there a divil stannin'
behind ye, back o' yer left shoulder there, an' givin'
th'orders? Is there?

William   And never at any time did I take a penny for
my pains. I didn't need money – I've never needed

money – my people were well-to-do, Hesther had a large dowry.

Mikey What's goin' on in an hour lek that? What's yer name? Is that blood inside ye, or some black juice from the lap o' the worst weasel ever spawned?

William After a couple of weeks, the procession of journalists ceased. I padlocked the door, shuttered the windows, put up a note warning off trespassers. That – rumour and calumny aside – is what took place.

Mikey The first Hag o' Hell Weasel, one eye in the middle of her brow –

William Still, where slander's concerned, there's no defence, is there? The stain is there. Can't be scrubbed out. Live with it.

Bridgie *is working the pinafore and smiling to herself.*

Bridgie My Susannah. Married a fool, livin' in Cork – now d'ye mind?

Mikey (*still to himself*) I never met no one fit t'explain them queschins te me.

Bridgie I wuddent a let that happen te her.

William (*to audience*) I've always found that woeful. The stain of slander can't be removed. Wash, scrub, scrape – you only heighten the stain. Innocence has nothing to do with the case. I did *not* take money, Bridgie, I did *not* take over the cottage. But it's claimed

I did. That is to say, there's stain. And shame. Live
with it.

Pause.

Bridgie (*to audience, coldly alert*) Only what was
Bridgie Cleary *doin'* there that night – waitin' for te be
made a herring of? That's another name, isn't it, for
'dittherum-dattherum' – *waitin' for to be made a
herring of.*

Pause. The vibes in the space suggest it's **Mikey**'*s turn to
offer something. First* **William** *focuses on him, not aggres-
sively, expectant rather. Then* **Bridgie** *directs her attention
likewise.* **Mikey** *reluctantly registers the temperature. His
response is to take off his cap, look down morosely into the
bowl of it, and fold it up. He sits with his head bowed,
staring at the folded cap and the unforgiving ground. He
looks up, some kind of ease entering him, some kind of
respite.*

Mikey Only two sounds in the world. Sound of a
scythe singin' ripe is the meado', sound o' the scythe
hittin' stone ...

SCENE NINE

Almost total blackout, a mini-interval of one minute's duration. The lights return to normal.

Resumption – **Mikey** *is downstage left, seated;* **William,** *stage left, seated;* **Bridgie** *is at the Singer, preoccupied, threading a needle. She has difficulty threading the needle, keeps missing the target by a hair's breadth, but she's enjoying the tussle.*

The wind snaps. The piano scales echo faintly, flippant this time.

William Tell us a story, Bridgie, will you?

Bridgie *shakes her head.*

William Why not, Bridgie?

Bridgie (*soberly*) Phildy Reddan used say, 'Stories only happens te them as is able te tell them.'

Mikey Maynin'?

Bridgie I asked him that. 'Story can't happen,' sez he, 'till yer able te tell it.'

William 'Story can't happen till yer able to tell it ...'

Mikey I *see* what he's at – I've a notion I see now what he's after ...

William Yes?

Mikey *won't develop the theme.* **Bridgie** *is moving on.*

Bridgie Mikey Cleary –

She goes to him and whispers. He listens. She withdraws.

Bridgie As a great favour, Mikey Cleary –

He looks at her, suspicious.

Bridgie Or a small favour. Or a middlin' favour. A 'grace-an'-favour'!

Mikey (*pointing to* **William**) For this Sham-Squire's amusement, is it?

Bridgie (*seductively*) No, no, nuthin' the lek o' that. For us all, te create pastime, recreation!

Mikey *eyes her.*

William We *are* in need of recreation here, the more you think about it ...

Mikey *eyes* **William**.

William Well, we can't play draughts, bowls, whist – can we?

Mikey They shudda given us a deck o' cards!

Bridgie (*with a siren tilt*) Well? Not often I asks anniethin' of anniebody, is it?

Pause.

Mikey   All right so.

Bridgie   An' thank ye kindly.

William   I'm goin' a-milkin', sir, she said!

Mikey *tidies himself in desultory fashion.* **Bridgie** *produces a long strip of white ribbon from the drawer of the Singer, which she dons as a stand-in bridal veil. She speaks to* **William**.

Bridgie   You're Father O'Brien, William. (*She slips off her ring and gives it to him.*) An' (*indicating* **Mikey**) we're a pair readyin' ourselves towards a weddin' shortly for to be.

Bridgie *fetches* **Mikey** *and leads him processionally towards the 'officiating priest'.*

Bridgie   Father Thady O'Brien, PP, VF – *VF*, be the way, maynes *Very Free* with the whiskey. No matter. Reverind O'Brien once upon a mornin' performs a marriage ceremony: here be the groom, here be the bride!

William (*holding the ring aloft*)   With this ring, I thee wed. Do you, Bridgie, do you, Mikey, ek settera, ek settera ...

Bridgie   We do. Mikey Cleary?

Mikey   Te be sure we do.

Mikey *puts the ring on* **Bridgie**'s *finger.*

Bridgie Thanks, Father. Here's (*miming*) a few pence for yer bother. Where's the hooley? Lashin's an' layvin's! There's droves, droves gathered in a kitchen up the road.

The happy couple walk back down the aisle.

William (*scattering blessings*) Benedictus ... Benedictus ... Pater noster ... Dominus, Dominus ... Per omnia per omnia singulo singularum ...

Mikey I mind it poured.

Bridgie Happy the wedding the rain teems on! Happy the funeral the sun –

William No excessive drinking, *please*. Remember your Temperance Oaths – Sanctus, Sanctus, ora pro nobis – *ora pro nobis*–

William *becomes the fiddler at the feast, the soundtrack backing him up with 'The Rakes of Mallow'.* **William**, *with zest, is working his well-rosined bow.* **Bridgie** *dances while* **Mikey**, *from a stationary position, stamps the floor.*

Bridgie (*miming flinging more coins*) Her that pays the piper!

Mikey D'ye remember there kem a delij o' rain?

Traffic halts.

Bridgie But it cleared towards evenin'. We went te Clonmel, didn't we, Mikey, stayed overnight – upstairs room of an aytin' house. Feather-bed, feather-bolster, big hairy Turk of a man stretched next me, thighs on him lek the side-boards of a plough, I thought I was a med woman. Sez I te meself, 'We're bin baptised all over again!'

Mikey   Med woman! *Med woman* – did ye now?

Bridgie   I thought, Bridgie, it's all before ye, all before ye lek the wheel of a barra!

Mikey (*revolts*)   Ye streel ye! (*He returns to his seat.*) Shuddent I have known damn well not te give ye yer head? What's Mikey Cleary – a scarcrow, is it, te flap in the wind of yeer jig-antics. Two of yiz in it – *streepach*!

Bridgie (*feckless*)   Commencin' ruction atween the Happy Couple!

Mikey   Nuthin' changes.

William   My dear Brethren – my dear Brethren –

Mikey   World o' boulders, nuthin' changes.

Bridgie   Fought before they were outa the chapel!

Mikey   Yev the same weather-cock head on ye as the first day I'd the bad luck te cross ye –

William   Just a tiff – lover's tiff – tear-an'-the-smile, Irish eyes, morn in spring –

Mikey   Ye Prodestan' horse-thievin' ditch-spawn bumbailiff's gombeen-man ould gistra, ye –

Bridgie (*swirling the space, in full flow*)   It was lek a chapter from a printed book, Father Thady, me *sagart aroon*, a printed book! With coloured pages an' curly lettrin' an' gilded covers – I saw it with me own two eyes, saw it all reportered in *The Clonmel Sentinel, The Thurles Clarion*, an' *The Freeman's Journal*, an' American papers please copy. There it was – whole story – plain as porpentine.

Mikey   Sit down, ye *smuiteen*, for Christ's sake, an' doan be makin' a sequestered Punch-an'-Judy of us before that mountebank, will ye? Mournin' Mother o' Christ, was it for this I was coffin'd?

Dead stop. Extend pause to maximum.

Bridgie (*to* **William**)   I'm sorry, Reverind O'Brien, heartily sorry for yer trouble, an' these caterwaulin's. Only don't ramble off, ye'll be needed for further sights an' ceremonies, hould yer hoult there.

Bridgie *speaks to* **Mikey**, *who is seething on the fringe.*

Mikey   Keep clear o' me, you – the two of yiz. I didn't land here to be med a jeer of be me sometime wife an' her fancy boy. Give over the pair of ye – I won't say it again.

Bridgie *takes off the ring and abandons it on the table.*

Bridgie   I'm sorry, sorry beyond all tellin', it fell out the way it did, but shure there y'are. Things happen an' then they can't *un*-happen, do what ye will, they can't *un*-happen. That's a chief sorrow o' the world, I discovered.

Mikey Ye wagon ye, I cud be back in me cooper's yard, watchin' yer wandrin' eyes starin' outa the winda – it's worse yer gettin', ye barge ye. I was never anniethin' more te ye nor cunt-fodder, an' well I knew it, was there anniewan didn't know it? Was there? *Answer me!*

Bridgie *is already back to* **William**, *miming giving him more money.*

Bridgie A few more shillin's, Father. Say a few prayers, would ye, for the dear departed – an' the dear te come – an', in special – are ye lisnin' now, *Sagart Aroon* –

William Certainly, I'm listening, Bridgie, tell me your needs.

Bridgie I want prayers in special for them that *nearly* breaks outa the shell, the trembly, the timid, that's often forgot about. Bridgie Cleary knows them all right – she knows them. (*To audience*) An' haven't youse, haven't youse all met them? The freckened wans that gets almos' all-the-way outa the shell an' then, for some rayzon – does the light hurt their eyes? courage fail them? some deloother occur? – for some rayzon they scrunch up, *frog in a frost*, sink inta quiet. Or worse, court calamtee, find it too – them is the ones, as menchin'd before, known be the name o' dittherum-dattherums, aye, the ones whose wings gets clogged in the shell.

Pause. **Bridgie** *is wounded but poised for her next jump.* **William** *is focused on Bridgie.* **Mikey**, *slapping ointment on his hands, is in some distress.*

Mikey Cunt-fodder, that was the land I got one fine day in the middle o' week; yer nuthin' more nor cunt-fodder, Mikey, for yer lawful wife Bridget Cleary an' her wandrin' eyes starin' outa that winda.

The ass brays again, only this time it's a tour de force, *an aria. As it hits its stride,* **William** *claps his hands over his ears.* **Bridgie** *half-smiles as she notices.* **Mikey** *is concentrating on his hands and the ointment. The bray fades melodiously.* **William** *still has his hands to his ears.* **Bridgie** *signals to him and he relaxes, suspicious.*

William Can't stand them, don't know why. Maybe one bit my mother before I was born.

Mikey (*undertone*) *Some*thin' bit her.

Bridgie (*seamlessly resuming her wedding motif*) I'm glad ye stayed, Father, an' pray God there's no hurry on ye cos we've a Second Wedding, as often happens in one guise or another. A Second Wedding shortly pealed its bells.

William Deo gratias!

Mikey An', by the bye, consarnin' the First Weddin', Mikey Cleary wasn't the one pushin' for the med match, he was dallamullogued inta it.

Bridgie A Second Wedding!

Mikey I belayve I was put spells on. I *know* I wasn't *in* meself.

William   Ora pro nobis! Dominus, Dominus ...

Bridgie   Listen te them pealin' bells ...

Mikey   An I'm led te th'altar quiet as a pet mouse.

Bridgie (*commanding the space*)   Second Nupchils
comin' roun'. It was quiet times, it was sudden times,
sudden times an' the heart un-aisy, the leaves fallin' an'
a swallow callin'. 'Sudden times, Bridgie Cleary, sudden
times.'

Mikey   I doan know who that woman is –

Mikey *gathers himself and walks out.*

Bridgie (*across the exit*)   God bless that poor man, he
always loved stormin out'.

She and **William** *listen for a beat of five. The storm cuts
loose with a savage ferocity.* **Mikey**, *battling against a force-
ten wind, reappears in a 'doorway'. He struggles back and
forth in the border zone. Finally the storm flings him back
into the space. He picks himself up and returns, bruised, to
his seat. The storm is long gone.*

Bridgie   Mikey Cleary, I will thank ye not te provoke
inclemen' weather for the Second Nupchils of yer
sometime wife Bridgie.

Mikey (*to himself*)   Bull in the mist ... Bull in the mist
...

Bridgie *turns to* **William**, *seats him, and sits on his knee.*

Bridgie Well, William Simpson, presentable idler an'
Landlord's Agent boycotted be all, you with them
lonesomes in yer eye, how do I look? Twenty-three,
dressmaker/mill'ner, bee-stung lips, rose in the cheeks,
an' (*singing*) *Me love-stone keeps bitin' away, away/Me
love-stone keeps bitin' away ...*'

Mikey Lek a bull run amuk in a mist ...

William *checks playfully.* **Mikey,** *with some deliberation,
removes his jacket and turns it inside out. He puts it on
again.*

William Sweet as a nut, Bridgie.

Bridgie An' you, William, game as a gander, an' I tuk
great pleasure in your sonsy comin's and goin's.

William Only one I ever loved, Bridgie, was you.

Bridgie Is that so?

William What happened, Bridgie?

Bridgie What happened?

William Broke my heart what happened.

Neutrally she caresses his cheeks and fondles his hair.

Bridgie I knows that, William –

William End of – everything, that was, for me.

Bridgie I knows that, *a chroí*. I knows ye loved Bridgie Cleary.

Mikey, *lidded ointment box in his possession, rises and goes on preoccupied patrol, touring the perimeter of the space. It's clear he's leaving* **Bridgie**'s *second wedding largely to its own fate.*

William We should have gone away together, Bridgie.

Bridgie Ye'd say so, William?

William That's what was waiting for us.

Bridgie The two of us away together, is it?

William You agreed once, I remember. You'd said, 'We'll go,' didn't you? I could tell you exactly where we were at the time – we were –

Bridgie William –

William Now you deny it?

Bridgie That cuddent have happened, William – we cuddent have gone away together –

William But you agreed to it that evening. I can tell you exactly where we were –

Bridgie Our bodies, William –

William Met. If ever bodies met.

Bridgie To be sure they met –

William I *know* they met.

Bridgie *Our bodies met like famished things/Our souls, our souls stayed separate things ...*

William Not true, Bridgie, not true, not true ...

Mikey *goes to an exit point, hurls the ointment box into the void, and resumes his patrol.*

Mikey Away with ye now an' plague someone else.

William I was never happier. A man boycotted, but that brought you to me. A man in love, a man loved, let it go on forever was my prayer, only get out of there, go abroad, be shut of them all, fall into our own lives, embrace our own lives ... Bridgie?

Bridgie (*not listening, she moves away from him*) The souls, the souls, William, not meant te mingle. Bodies met, aye, an' sweat mingled. *But for our souls, our souls brushed wings.* No blame, no blame. I knows, all knows well th'insurmountables o' lovers' achin's. Vow an' sigh returns te haunt. Are ye lisnin' there, Mikey Cleary? (**Mikey** *is back in his seat, brooding.*) This is for you too. This is for all consarned, cos what's strayed from the accounts is Bridgie's story is a Love Story, which fact needs te be roundly stated. These is not trivyel matters, thank you. (*To audience.*) My thanks to all comers for attention yielded.

William Bridgie –

Mikey   Give over, William.

Bridgie   It tuk me a while te puzzle it out. The Spin o'
Love – if it's ordnary, if it's God-send-Sunday, ye might
as well be warmin' yer arse to a whin-bush. Love story
that matters is a kindled jewel an' ever will be. An' so,
an' so, from William o' the Second Nupchils, Bridgie
Cleary turned away, an' set forth for her Venture on
The Low Road in what shudda been the mornin'
gleam – only turned out, as is now well-known,
reportered in all the papers, turned out to be the yalla,
lackaday yalla, o' the evenin' sun ...

Pause. The lighting alters. A spot, forming slowly, settles on
Bridgie. *She's at the Singer, reprising her 'earrings' cameo,
but now wearing the ribbon bridal veil. She is fragile,
ambiguous, vulnerable, bride.* **Mikey** *and* **William**, *scarcely
visible, are trapped in their habitual stations on the margins.*

Bridgie (*lightly touching the earrings*)   Them earrings –
much admired – Phildy Reddan, Egg-Man, bosom-
frien' o' the low road, who had a wisdom from walkin'
early, quick dew still on the grass, Phildy was the man
gev me them earrings last time we lay together, joined
cons'mately, as was our wont, an', across his final an'
lastin' kiss, sez he, 'Tek care, Bridgie, the minit passin'
an' not returnin'.'

She takes the blue hanky from her pocket and plays with it.

Bridgie   What kind ov a man was he, me bosom-frien'
an' lover an' golden plover o' the low road? I'll tell yiz –
he knew Bridgie Cleary, he cud read that lassie's map.
'How's it ye can read me map so well?' 'I larned that

from the women.' 'They gev ye them hands too?' 'Te be sure – the supple breasts o' limber women.' 'An' the flame in them eyes?' 'You gev me that, Bridgie.' 'Is there a shada in ye at all, Phildy Reddan?' 'Bandit acres o' shada, *a chroí* ...' 'What am I doin' so in th'arms of a livin' danger?' 'Two of us in it, Bridgie. You're bright as midsummer *an'* a river o' shada. That's why we're talkin'. That's what has the townlands talkin'. They're *afeared*, Bridgie.' 'Why're they afeared?' 'They're afeared we'll *be*, Bridgie, *they're afeared we'll be.*'

Mikey (*to anyone*)   I reckenise ye now, it's you that's in it, Bridgie.

Bridgie   'Why're they afeared we'll *be*, Phildy?' 'They're livin' be rules mostly, Bridgie, you an' me is seekin' te live be the light 'ithin. Hard for people, Bridgie, freckens people, when the leks o' you an' me decides te go after the light 'ithin.'

She relaxes, plays with the ribbon veil on her head, and rises from the Singer with the hanky in her hand. The wind whines, snaps, and moans. She wanders (spot is diffuse, gradually extending) to an exit point, looks out, and steadies herself.

Bridgie (*fiercely into the void*)   Phi-llllllll-dy!

No response. Reprise. No response. Defiant second reprise. Beat. She starts, and joy takes possession of her. He's coming. He's (invisible) in her arms. She caresses him, mutters endearments, love sounds coming from her. Beat.
    Holding the blue hanky aloft (lamp lighting tuned accordingly) she leads Phildy downstage to meet the 'family'.

She visits **Mikey** *and* **William** *in turn, the hanky-lamp lighting the way.*

    Bridgie *now dances with her invisible partner, the hanky-lamp still providing illumination.*

Bridgie Hag o' the air or homeless fairy/Or were ye spouse te Mikey Cleary?/No, nay, never a witch, never a fairy/Was wance wedded to a man called Cleary ... Sometime fresh, more often weary/I sought a lover'd treat me fairly/Step forward, William, bright an' early/An' show yer a match for Bridgie Cleary ... William, William, bright an' early/Gathered himself, shoulders squarely/Bodies met, souls but rarely/Ould hungers lingered in Bridgie Cleary ... But in Phildy Reddan from Coroneary/The woman found what she longed for dearly/Body te savour, an' not that merely/A buxom soul-mate for Bridgie Cleary.

Kiss. Embrace. Pause.

William I loved her because she was disturbed ...

Bridgie *(with hints of* deraciné*)* The door, the door, that door I spoke of in the side of Slievenamon – 'The Spotty Door' – go through there yer with Th' Other Crowd – take a blasht from them an' mebbe never come back ...

William Isn't that odd?

Mikey She wasn't disturbed.

Bridgie *(to anyone)* But thought came te me wance – still does – if yer in love, an' able te meet the calls, the legend summons o' love, ye cud go through that door, luk around, an' come back unharmed, because if yer in love, an', as I say, has the courage o' love's demands, then ye can go anniewhere, do anniethin'. All awaits, all is, an' all will be ...

Mikey   Bridgie –

William   Being boycotted was the happiest time of my life.

Mikey   Why din't ye walk down the road with him?

Bridgie *wanders upstage towards an exit, the hanky-lamp still an item. She stands poised, listening intently, and the others listen also. Only the silence answers.*

Bridgie (*from upstage position*)   That silence out there ... if it wasn't for a colour in the silence out there, I believe I'd say good-bye te me moorin's.

Pause.

William   'You've no belief in th'Unvisible,' Bridgie always said. 'That's your bother, William Simpson.'

Pause.

Mikey   Why din't ye pack yer duds, Bridgie, an' away wi' the pair o' ye?

William   She changed her mind, that's all.

Mikey But *why'd she change her mind* – I believe I
knows the why.

Bridgie *is back at the Singer. She pockets the blue hanky
and takes the ribbon veil from her hair. She looks at it in a
wash of grief. During the upcoming speech she winds the
ribbon about her index finger, with combustible decorum,
into a compact ball of white.*

Bridgie I tuk fright. Seemed te me, I cuddent breathe
without that man. Then, of a suddent, I'm freckened –
everythin' chaff in me mouth. I'd said, 'Yes, *a chroí*,' an'
we're ready for the road. Cork was the plan. We'd the
money saved. He knew droves beyant in New York –
we'd have med our way. The day comes. Bridgie
Cleary, lassie in love for the first time in her born days
– (**Mikey** *shakes his head*) sits there. Can't stir.
Everythin' chaff in her mouth.

Pause. The heron sounds. With automatic hands **Bridgie**
*continues winding the ribbon into a secure ball. The heron
fades.*

Bridgie An' why was that? I was the same wan –
wasn't I? – that over the months, a year, say, stretched
beside him, blended with him, schemed departure.
Susannah, I mind, kem by – sun in the liver o' the sky.
I med some escuse, druv her away – yes, I did that. I
sat there in th'expandin' quiet. Dog kem in, cat kem
in, druv them out of it too.

*Pause. The ribbon is a neat ball of white resting in her
hand. She studies it bleakly, looks at the audience. The
lighting tends to isolate her again.*

Bridgie An' the bother? Me life – what's always the bother. Me arranged life, mesh of it, there in that place. Mikey me husban', William down the road, Susannah, me father foostherin' aroun', the mother keepin' an eye from her hill-graveyard. (*Pause.*) Unremarkable things ruz up – customers, orders, shape of a bush, fresh face o' the fields, April comin', Slievenamon – all tuk hould o' me. Dog whinin' at the door, clock noisy on the dresser, man I loved waitin' at the spot agreed. I cuddent stir. No wan te hobble me, I'm in chains. An' worse, worst of all, knew te the far ends o' me bones the cost o' this 'prisonment – I wasn't spared that afflickshin, an' rightly so. I cud hear his voice, his uttered warnin', it scoured me te the marra – 'Tek care, Bridgie, tek care the minit passin' – an' not returnin'.'

Coda. Lighting changes to carry transition. **Mikey** *is seated, studying the cap as he holds it at arm's length looking into the bowl of it, viewing it as it rests on the floor.* **Bridgie** *is by the Singer. She is thoughtfully 'playing the piano'.* **William** *is seated, but full of motion. He rises and gathers his belongings, including the mirror which he had hung on the 'wall' earlier.*

Bridgie Goin' somewhere?

William (*to* **Mikey**) Why did you turn your coat that way?

Mikey A pishogue.

Bridgie If you stan' on a stray-sod, lose yer way, turn yer coat inside out. They say it'll help ye find yer way home ...

William (*to* **Mikey**) Every good wish, Mikey. (*He turns to* **Bridgie**.) Glad to have met you again, Bridgie, I ... I ...

He shakes his head in confusion, surrender. He exits, stepping out bravely/foolishly. **Mikey** *and* **Bridgie** *listen, curious. Silence.*

Mikey No storm t'attack *him*, mind ye!

Bridgie Playin' with him, they are ...

Mikey Ye'd say?

Bridgie Just playin' him ...

Beat.

Mikey Never changed, did he?

Bridgie Hardest thing ....

Mikey Near as bad a liar as meself.

Bridgie All of us has our lies, swathes of them, all of us.

Mikey An' no sheddin' them? Is there no sheddin' them, Bridgie?

Bridgie (*elsewhere*) William, God bless him, can't stand the bawl of an ass ...

Mikey *takes to touring the space, his next move coming to* *the boil slowly, rapidly.* **Bridgie** *sits there, knowing what's coming. A point of tension is reached in* **Mikey**'s *patrolling when the rhythm must break.* **Mikey** *stumbles to* **Bridgie** *and falls on his knees, head bowed before her.*

Mikey Touch me, Bridgie. Touch me, touch me, touch me, Jesus, touch me, will ye? May I never rise from this if ye won't touch me, clane me, rid me for good an' all o' what I dun te ye. I let the worst thing enter, Bridgie, enter and possess me, I changed te the worst thing, tuk up the paraffin, burnt ye inta the clay ...

Pause. She reaches, touches him, forgiveness in her touch. He rises and looks at her.

Mikey I loved ye – ye see ...

Bridgie Yes, I knows that.

Mikey Never stopped lovin' ye.

Mikey *reaches, hesitant. There is a lifetime's veto in the hesitation. He reaches, touches her.*

Bridgie I knows that.

Mikey *on patrol again. He halts.*

Mikey (*pleading*) Wasn't yer first time in love, Bridgie, Phildy Reddan –

Bridgie *attends.*

Mikey I knew ye in love long before annie o' that, Bridgie ... us two in love ...

Pause.

Bridgie I'll tell ye how it was, Mikey. Once upon a time I fell in love with a purty man. (*Pause.*) Eternally I see him, eternally returnin' ...

*Enter **William**, stricken **William**. He goes to his position and sits, exhausted.*

William I met a man out there. 'Who're you?' he enquired. 'William Simpson,' I said. 'The Liar Simpson?' he asked. 'Is it The Liar Simpson I have before me?' I said nothing for a long time. Then I answered, 'Yes. The Liar Simpson.'

Long pause.

Mikey Yer welcome back, William.

Bridgie Rest yerself there.

*Pause. **William** settles in his customary mooring. The Singer whirrs into independent life, does its dance with **Bridgie** quietly conducting. It whirrs to a stop.*

Bridgie Time this lassie did a bit o' work ...

__Mikey__ looks at his hands. He starts, with a tint of the therapeutic to the action, clapping one hand deliberately against the other, at intervals checking the palms. Bridgie is moving about the space. She mimes plucking various

*materials from invisible shelves (to accompany the verbal
score), feeling the material, tossing it –* propriétaire *in the
gesture – aside.* **Mikey**'s *continuing hand claps, as matters
develop, find a niche as punctuation marks in the context
of her riff.*

Bridgie Gossamer ... Gossamer ... Silk ... Raw silk ...
Slubbed silk, slubbed silk. Sarsenet, sarsenet for linin's
– te captingate the quality. An' velvet, velvety stuff,
velvet gown there – d'ye mind the *pile* o' that velvet ...
An' velveteen, velveteen, velveteen for gamekeepers'
britches – to defend their hams from the brambles!

Mikey Gossamer –

Bridgie Yes – there's a hat, remember, we called a
'gossamer' –

Mikey No, no, but the fields, them cobwebs ...

Bridgie Cobwebs!

Mikey Aye, in the fields, roun' Michaelmas –

Bridgie Cobwebs! No but *gossamer*, Mikey Cleary,
don't go makin' that mistake, gossamer on a slope o'
mornin' has nuthin' te do with yer ruin o' cobwebs
behind a dresser or drapin' rafters of a barn. Meet
gossamer, ye know that much. An' I met true gossamer.
Thank ye, Mikey Cleary. They can't take that from me.

Bridgie *goes to the Singer and starts work on the shirt.*
William *goes on perturbed patrol.* **Mikey** *settles, takes off a
boot, foosters with it, puts it on again. Everything seems*

back to normal. The play is clearly about to end, but wait, **Mikey** *has another thought for us, for himself, for us ...*

Mikey Bull in a mist, bull in a mist ...

Bridgie *is working on the shirt.* **William** *is on patrol.* **Mikey** *keeps a troubled eye on that bull in the mist. Slow fade to blackout. End.*